SUCCESS
GRAVITY

7 Keys to unlock Your Dream Lifestyle

EPI MABIKA

www.fast-print.net/store.php

ISBN: 978-178035-680-8

Cover design & layout by David Springer

First published 2013 by
Fastprint Publishing
Peterborough, England.

An environmentally friendly book printed and bound in England by
www.printondemand-worldwide.com

This book is made entirely of chain-of-custody materials

'Success Gravity'
is also available as an unabridged
audiobook and digital e-book.
More copies can be ordered at
www.successgravity.com;
www.amazon.com
and all good book stores.

Dedication

To my Two Greatest Heroes on whose
shoulders I stand today!

To Mum: In Honour of You

In carrying my candle, I carry yours too, to light up the world in places of darkness. I walk tall today because I stand on your shoulders, building upon the foundation you have laid for me.

You are such a strong pillar of wisdom and light upon my life- a constant source of encouragement. Nothing compares to a mother's love. I cherish your presence, the strong bond and support you tirelessly give to me, I love you with all my heart. Until a better word can be found to express my utmost and sincere gratitude, 'Thank You' will have to do.

For believing in me, giving me life, an education and a great platform in helping me become the success I am today. Your relentlessness and determination continue to motivate me to never give up on my dreams. Today I confidently lean on your teachings that have catapulted me into my destiny, causing me to fly high and soar above the winds.

I am richly blessed with the mandate and responsibility of bearing your name. What an honour, what a delight it is, to be called your daughter!

To me you are and will always be-

My Mother - My Teacher - My Friend.

To Dad: In Memory of You

To us: A Faithful father. To Mum: A Loving Husband.
To the world: A devout Man of Great Stature and
Integrity.

Sing with the angels. The song you first taught me
to believe in my dreams, I sing it too. You gave me
the lyrics, I sing my own tune. You are always there
because I carry your genes within me. The wisdom
you profoundly imparted to me is harnessed in my
favour as life demands. I'm eternally grateful that
the Lord lent you to us. What a prize, what a vessel,
what an honour it is to have been connected to you!
The times we shared, the memories made, are forever
engraved upon my heart.

The depth of your love is forever rooted in me, while
the fragrance of your peace lingers on. The richness
of your kindness amazes me to this day. Your legacy
lives on Daddy.

You did not live in vain, because in sharing my message, I share yours too, and indeed in my heart I echo
those words so richly engraved on Isaac Newton's
monument: "Mortals rejoice that there has existed
such and so great an ornament to the human race".
In our world you are a hero and I know that your soul
rests in eternal peace because that is what your life
stood for: Love and Peace always.

The Last of Your Very Precious Seed.

Acknowledgements

God my creator: For embedding this book assignment inside me and recognising that the hour is now ripe to bring it into manifestation for such a time as this. I thank You and give all glory and honour to You.

Family members: Regis, Boniface, Priscilla, Juliet and Ruth. Just by being in my life, you have all richly contributed towards the success of this book. Thank You for your unwavering love and support.

Bishop Wayne Malcolm: The passion to pursue my dream in writing this book has been ignited under your tutorage. You are indeed a great role model for success. Thank you for being the champion nurturer that you are.

Victor Granville: You have been instrumental in helping to pull this book out of me. Thank you for being the 'coach extraordinaire' that you are.

X

Contents

Preface   XIII
Introduction   XIX

Chapter 1:   GOALS   **27**

  1)   Write Goals Down, To Tie Them Up!   27
  2)   The Big 'Y'   32
  3)   Use Deadlines As Lifelines   35
  4)   Be "Eco-Friendly": Recycle Goals   40

Chapter 2:   RELATIONSHIPS   **47**

  1)   Friend or Foe: What Are You To YOU?   47
  2)   Fellows, Foes, Family, Friends:
     The Survival Tool Kit   51
  3)   Your Network Determines Your Net worth   55
  4)   The Big Shift: Competition to Collaboration   58

Chapter 3:   ATTITUDE   **65**

  1)   Your Attitude Determines Your Altitude   66
  2)   The Past Is Past: Harvest The Lessons   69
  3)   Battlefield Of The Mind   73
  4)   Perception Is Reality   77

Chapter 4:   VISION   **85**

1)   Put On Your Senses! Sight vs Vision   84
2)   Avatar: Choose Your Reality   89
3)   Visualisation: A Modern Art Phenomenon   93
4)   Imagination Is The Limitation   96

Chapter 5:   INTEGRITY   **101**

1)   Lifeblood Of The Body   102
2)   Last Man standing   106
3)   Apparently Transparent   110
4)   Three Musketeers: Legal, Ethical, Moral   113

Chapter 6:   TIME MANAGEMENT   **119**

The 4 P's
1)   Powerful Perishable Resource   120
2)   Procrastinate Procrastination!   122
3)   Proper Prior Planning Prevents
     Poor Performance   124
4)   Productivity: The Pareto Principle   128

Chapter 7:   YOUR CONTRIBUTION   **135**

1)   Show Me Your Birth Certificate!   136
2)   Legacy: Live It To Leave It   138
3)   Immortality: Your Best Shot Beyond
     The Grave   141
4)   Success To Significance   142

Conclusion   149

SUCCESS
G R A V I T Y

Preface

This book is a map and blueprint with a tried, tested and proven formula for achieving success. Having done over 10 years of study on this subject, I have found that there are various expressions to the success formula, with the theoretical terms coined differently, however, the underlying principles are essentially the same. You will find an offering in this book, with a more practical guide from experiential knowledge as well as indepth research from experts who have achieved success on multiple levels. Having applied these principles myself and seen phenomenal results, I have realised the importance of condensing the truths that I have discovered into a book that will serve you well and shorten the learning curve for your success.

THE CONCEPT OF GRAVITY IS THREE-FOLD:

1. GRAVITY is primarily an acronym for Goals; Relationships; Attitude; Vision; Integrity; Time management, and Your contribution. These are the seven keys that I explore, using my own experiences and also evidence from others who have applied these principles and achieved the success results that they desired. The simplicity of the acronym makes it memorable and easy to apply at any stage during the success process, so you can stop and ask yourself at any time: Do I have the right connections? Are my goals realistic? Do I have a clear picture of what I want? Am I confessing the right things over my life? What skills do I require? Am I procrastinating? Who's help do I need? What sort of impact do I want to make in this area? The answers to questions like these can begin to serve as signposts to put you on your desired success pathway.

2. Secondly, the Paradox of Gravity serves to encourage 'Divergent Thinking', which is necessary for CREATIVITY, INNOVATION and ultimately SUCCESS. It is not enough just to think; it is important to challenge the popular logic, status quo, conditioning and social hypnosis that we are continually exposed and accustomed to, in order to bring about success. This involves a paradigm shift from the common negative connotation of gravity pulling you down, to

accepting it as a good and inevitable force
that keeps you grounded and firmly rooted to
establish longevity and stability in success. For
it is this kind of tangible, steadfast success that
keeps you from chasing an 'elusive illusion'.
As an Analogy, if you take a look at a party helium
balloon, you will find that it floats away without
a grip or a weight on it. Being filled with helium
gas that is lighter and less dense than air, it floats
above the air and in essence is non-compliant
with gravity because it has no weightiness to
it. However, the decorative purpose of a party
helium balloon finds its necessity here on the
earth, and not up in the air somewhere. In much
the same way, you want success that holds
down, that is tangible and can be passed on from
generation to generation because it is grounded.
It has substance and value within it, not the
kind that is fleeting or elusive. Success serves
its purpose when it is within grasp where it is
applicable in your life and in the lives of other
people around you right here, right now, and not
someday later because as you know, "someday"
is not on the calendar!
Furthermore, the unpredictable nature of
this book theme violates expectancy, making
it more intriguing as it is not what one would
automatically assume. It increases inquisitiveness
and subconsciously causes you to adopt this
prescriptive pattern to apply to your own
thinking process, thereby unleashing creativity.
Each compound of this formula is in turn related

to the concept of gravity to help you to attain Grounded Success, forming the basis for the whole ethos behind the book and its title.

3. Lastly, yes, as you may have gathered from the title, Sir Isaac Newton does have a say in all this, having discovered the scientific concept of the 'Law of Gravity'. In its simplest expression, gravity can be defined as "a force that attracts objects to all other objects". With Gravity being a Central Magnetic Force, parallels can thus be drawn from the 'Law of Attraction' to demonstrate how these proven principles of success inevitably work together in your favour if you work with them. In essence, it's about how to work with gravity as opposed to working hard against it, to produce desired results. Seeing as there is no need to re-invent the wheel, the wise choice is to work with what has been proven to work.

Incidentally, the inscription on Sir Isaac Newton's monument, located in London's Westminster Abbey, is very profound. The Italian translation reads as follows: "Mortals rejoice, that there has existed such and so great an ornament to the human race". Wow! What a testimonial!!! I am therefore challenging you the reader to create a lifestyle that ensures that those words or similar, ring true for you when you depart from this world. This calls for devising a 'Legacy Building Framework' with a Paradigm Shift from just mere Success to Significance. Next, you arrive at that pinnacle point where you ultimately discover that Significance really is the gravitational pull behind true and lasting Success.

Just like gravity is an inevitable force, success too becomes inevitable if these principles are applied. Notice I didn't say affirmed, believed or understood, but ... APPLIED! I'm talking about inescapable, limitless, boundless, grounded success that causes you to come from obscurity to significance. In writing the book, I have also embarked on my own significance journey hence 'walking the talk'.

If you allow it, this book will become a 'midwife' for you to help birth the dreams inside of you that are waiting to be unleashed. With this enlightenment, give yourself permission to be, to do and to have all you ever want to in this one and only precious lifetime that you have. Maximise and make the utmost out of it! You owe it to yourself, your Creator, and those whom you have been called to serve and influence in this generation and beyond.

Introduction

The dawning of the recession brought about an awakening to the clarion call for creativity and innovation as an adjunct to traditional methods of occupation, as asserted by Wayne Malcolm. The idea of Job dependence has become conspicuously obsolete, and I believe there is a much higher need now for individuals to connect to their purpose in order to successfully create the lifestyle of their dreams to sustain them. Entrepreneurship has now become a necessary career path, and for some, a very different way to think and work. In this new economy, an entrepreneurial mind makes it possible to create true, lasting, grounded success that is built around your values and lifestyle choices. Resourcefulness has therefore become paramount as you strive for employability as opposed to just seeking employment or acquiring resources. You now need to make yourself an indispensable asset, not just a mere option for someone to choose, skip or make redundant.

A stay at home mum, for instance, doesn't have to be torn between looking after her children and finding a job to pursue a pay cheque that supplements her income. She can have the best of both worlds by creating a home based business that she will enjoy while supporting her lifestyle choices. Simple examples include offering online tuition on her expertise, becoming a virtual assistant, or starting a home-based cake baking business. On the other hand, those stuck in volatile corporate jobs that they hate can begin to tap into their true purpose and go after their dream career, or start a business that will satisfy them and also support their dream lifestyle. According to the Forbes Employee Satisfaction Survey Report (2012), the statistics show that an alarming 65% of working adults aged between 25-40 are finding that they are stuck in jobs that they totally detest. The job therefore serves just to pay the bills, while work life is empty and they are just hanging in there so they can retire and finally do what they love to do. You need to realise that your occupation is a central component to a well-lived life. It goes without saying that if you work eight hours a day, this is equivalent to spending a third of your day at work. If you sleep an average of eight hours a night, that only leaves you with eight hours to travel to and from work, cook, clean, relax, catch up with loved ones and live your life! You end up realising that most of your conscious day is spent at work, so your occupation really should connect to your purpose in order for you to enjoy your life.

A turning point in my life was when I discovered that I was responsible for my life. I knew there had to be more to life than just the mediocrity of routine, the varying vicissitudes of circumstances, and the mundane motions that we go through in life. The outcome of all this was really up to me. So as life happened,

I realised that I had a choice as to how I would respond to it in order to make it enjoyable. Furthermore, I could actually become proactive and dictate what consequences and experiences I could encounter in my life by living it on purpose and by design. Wow, that was a big game changer for me, empowering me to take full ownership of life, realising that it is not a stage rehearsal for something else! It is the real thing, the actual play, and I am the main character! The acceptance of personal responsibility is the first stage and theme for successful people. After this, your whole life begins to change and take the shape that you mould it to be. You become proactive about life, and not reactive, as you start to live your life by design. All skills necessary for success are learnable, whether it is in business, sales, money, relationships or life itself. What thousands of people have done, you can do also.

You will find that intertwining the seven GRAVITY components in this book ensures that they can now be woven to bring out the best tapestry unique to you, ultimately becoming your fingerprint picture of success. Each part works in sync with the others, so if one area is out of line, then you are out of balance for grounded success and stability. The magnitude of success is in direct proportion to the extent to which these principles are applied. In science, for instance, we know that depending on the proportions of ingredients used, you either get medicine or poison. It is therefore important to use calculated and tailor made quantities in order to achieve a successful balance.

Likewise, as a cake requires all the necessary ingredients to taste good, these principles should be meshed in correct proportions to bring about grounded success. You may then flavour and decorate a cake according to your personal style and optional preferences, meaning the ultimate picture of success should be your own definition of it in order to gratify your chosen desire. The pieces of the puzzle you want to create should all come from your chosen mental picture. Using pieces handed to you by others often causes frustration as you may work so diligently to complete the puzzle, only to find that the picture is not what you really desired.

Earl Nightingale defined success simply as 'a progressive realisation towards a worthy ideal'. That's all it is. It's neither houses, cars, nor a fat bank account. Those are just symbols that society has shaped and incorporated into a generic reflection of success, but that's not necessarily the case. One could have a fancy, expensive car and still not be successful. I had a flashy, hard top convertible 'coupe cabriolet' before on hire purchase, and always had nervous breakdowns each month before making the payments, for they were painfully exorbitant! I was in debt up to my eyeballs yet I wasn't successful, although one might say I had the symbol of success.

Today, from the free side of debt, getting a parking ticket for example, is just a mere inconvenience as opposed to the 'doctor's appointment for stress therapy' that it used to be. Financial success on my terms is 'peace of mind when paying bills and living expenses'. In fact, I look forward to it now because it's all in the budget! It is also the ability to give and make a difference in someone else's life whilst simultaneously being able to fulfil my own dreams and desires.

The 'Gravity Message' for success rests on the premise that everything starts with a goal, and ends with a contribution. As you become what it takes for you to achieve those goals, you begin to realise that you can also make it happen for others and that is the highest achievement. After all, there is no true success without succession.

True success in and of itself is not an end but a means to an end, a journey and not a destination. When you can pass the baton on to others, you ensure that your place is history is secure. Your mark is made, and your story is told for generations to come. It's about shifting from an 'Inheritance' to 'Legacy' paradigm, implying that it's not so much what you can get, but rather what you can 'give back and leave' that counts for success, - the kind of Grounded Success that makes you significant.

'Mortals
rejoice that there
has existed such
and so great an
ornament to the
human race'

Monument Inscription for Isaac Newton

SUCCESS GRAVITY

7 Keys to unlock Your Dream Lifestyle

EPI MABIKA

'The tragedy in life doesn't lie in not reaching your goal. The tragedy lies in having no goal to reach.'

SUCCESS GRAVITY

CHAPTER 1

Goals

The Oxford English dictionary defines a goal as the result or achievement toward which effort is directed.

Goals envelop anything you would like to become, do or have in your life. This encompasses all the eight areas of what is called the 'Wheel of life': 1) physical - health, fitness, nutrition, appearance; 2) personal finances - money, debt management, financial freedom; 3) career, vocation, business; 4) personal growth and development; 5) social - fun and recreation; 6) family and friends; 7) relationships and romance, and 8) community - social contribution.

Your life begins to become a great life when you clearly identify what it is that you want, make a plan to achieve it and then work on that plan every single day. In the absence of clearly defined goals, we become strangely loyal to performing daily acts of trivia.

A goal is also synonymous with a dream. A Chinese proverb asserts that, "If you cannot dream, why should you sleep, and if you cannot pursue your dreams, why should you wake up?" Interesting food for thought there! Well, in the mind of Jim Rohn, 'The ultimate reason for setting goals is to entice you to become the person it takes to achieve them'.

The tragedy in life doesn't lie in not reaching your goal. The tragedy lies in having no goal to reach.

People who set goals achieve more in less time. Statistics show that 95% of people who set goals are likely to accomplish them. Goals should be clear, specific, detailed and measurable.

Be willing to give up who you've been, in order to give birth to who you can become. Albert Einstein said, "Life is like riding a bicycle. In order to keep your balance, you must keep moving." And Thomas Edison observed: "Many of life's failures are people who did not realise how close they were to success when they gave up". He also said, "Our greatest weakness lies in giving up. The most certain way to succeed is always to try just one more time". Napoleon Hill similarly stated that "the primary reason for failure is that people do not develop new plans to replace those plans that didn't work".

What you desire in life should be defined by you, and goals must be the first piece of the puzzle to complete the big picture. You cannot allow your life's trajectory to be decided by someone else, no matter how important they are. Take full ownership and responsibility for your own life. Live life on your terms, not on those of your parents, teachers, spouses, siblings, friends, mentors, peers or boss!

I)   WRITE GOALS DOWN, TO TIE THEM UP!

Writing down your goals begins to marshal energies that send your subconscious search engine to work to find those things you desire. It tends to tap deeper resources and draw the best out of life. This is the 'mystery' behind the Law of attraction. Your actions and results will gravitate towards your most dominant thoughts; therefore, write down and meditate on positive thoughts. As you think, so you become. Goals create a sense of mission and focus, which in turn lead to concentration of power and attraction of resources to make that goal a reality.

Putting it in writing breathes life into a goal, giving it legs and making you an unstoppable force. You must write down your goal as if you were placing an order from a menu at a restaurant. For example, just as you might order a medium rare sirloin steak, or a tall, skinny, wet, extra hot latte with no cream from Starbucks, so too must you be specific in spelling out your goals.

They need to be written down as writing brings commitment and a reference point in the future when it is required. It helps bring clarity of purpose, intent and result. Writing goals also releases energies, that will not only heighten awareness, but also erect mental antennae in preparation to pick up any signals in relation to a particular goal. This is what scientists call the Reticular Activation System - RAS for short. It is a personal pilot light for success and is an area within your brain that filters information that has some importance to you, raising awareness of what you need to pay attention to.

So for example, in the middle of a noisy crowded room, if someone mentions your name, you seem to hear it from nowhere. Also, the all too familiar instance of when you are thinking of buying a new car, say for instance a red Toyota, all of a sudden, you will start noticing more red Toyotas on the road. The thing is they have always been there, but not brought to your attention prior to this because there was no conscious desire or link to notice them.

Sitting between the conscious and the subconscious mind, the RAS enables you to shut out what is not important so that you are not processing every piece of information presented to you, for instance noise from traffic. The ability to programme this filter through the conscious mind gives the RAS its importance in goal achievement.

This is where something is moved from the sub-conscious to the conscious mind and the sub-conscious goes to work to find things that will aid that goal to become a reality. This in turn is brought to your conscious mind for you to act on it, and then eventually, achievement takes place all because of the power of writing the goal down. Writing down goals has therefore been scientifically and psychologically proven to be half the battle won.

The RAS, however, is not able to make a distinction between a real and perceived stimulus or event, hence the chances of programming it by creating specific goals in your imagination are possible, particularly if they are sensory specific. It tends to 'believe' whatever message you give it. The filter then raises your awareness to items that can assist you in achieving your goals. Relevant information is therefore brought to our attention that would have otherwise remained as 'background noise'. By constantly meditating upon your goals, talking, writing and reviewing your goals, you reinforce the filter's programming.

Having a personal strong reason why you want to achieve a particular goal also serves as an anchor and pull factor to make you want to complete it.

Napoleon Hill asserted that we can achieve any realistic goal if we keep on thinking of that goal, and stop thinking any negative thoughts about it. Of course, if we keep thinking that we can't achieve a goal, our subconscious will help us NOT achieve it.

2) THE BIG 'Y'

Having a strong personal reason why you want to achieve a particular goal also serves as an anchor and pull factor to make you want to complete it. This is what I call the Big 'Y'. By way of example, you may decide you want to adopt a healthier lifestyle by going to the gym, or running two rounds in the park at least twice a week, drinking water before each meal and eating organic foods as much as possible. You would then monitor this by weighing yourself every month for six months with your ideal weight written down. The big reason why, could be that you want to live long enough to see your children's children, and play with them. This becomes a stronger gravitational pull towards success in achieving that goal, rather than just simply wanting to keep fit. If you can sell yourself well on the big picture and benefits, then you are most likely going to 'stick it out' when the going gets tough or in moments of low motivation.

In saying all this, persistence becomes of utmost importance, in order to avoid resistance stopping you in your track. Muhammad Ali put it this way: "It isn't the mountains ahead to climb that wear you out, but the pebble in your shoe". Therefore, persist through every small obstacle along the path to your goal achievement.

Here are the top five general reasons why you should set goals: Firstly, you will have more CLARITY. Setting goals requires you to develop clarity. You need to know where you want to go in order to get there. This is the first and most important step to creating a life that you love and want. Secondly, you will develop a stronger sense of FOCUS. You get more of what you focus on. If you have clear goals and focus on them, you will get more of what you DO want and less of what you don't want. Thirdly, when you are clear about where you want to go, you set up steps and actions to get there, thereby increasing your EFFICIENCY because you are working on what is really important. When you work on what's important, you will accomplish more than you expected. Fourthly, as you set out and reach your goals, you become more confident in your ability to do what you say and get what you want in life, resulting in increased SELF-CONFIDENCE. Success breeds more successes. Finally, RESULTS are achieved! This comes about as you focus on goals in every area of your life to maximise your potential.

Goals must be big! Daniel Burnham said, "Make no little plans for they have no magic to stir men's blood". There is no point in playing small and setting reachable obvious goals that don't require any stretching on your part. Goals within your comfort zone are not goals at all - they are just tasks to be completed. Goals should give you a kick and drive to want to achieve them. They should entice you to become the person you need to become in order to achieve them. For example, having a goal of being able to tie up your shoe laces is incredible for a child but not for an adult.

The richest place on the planet is not the banks or gold mines - it is the cemetery, because there lies all the potential that was never released. Some people die at 20, only to be buried at 90. Why? They embrace an aimless life by allowing their dreams to die within them. They cease to live and just start coasting through life, choosing to merely exist. Don't become one of them! Dreams and goals bring vitality to life. Imagine on your death bed, and surrounding you is not all your loved ones as would be ideal, but instead, all the ideas, businesses and inventions and they are staring angrily at you saying "we were depending on you to give us expression on this earth, now we must die with you!" How would you feel?

We don't serve the world by playing small. We all have a divine purpose and mandate that is huge and it seeks expression from you. This must be discovered, developed and deployed here and now.

Goals must be Big, Hairy, Audacious Goals (BHAG) that are beyond your reach and comfort zone: all that you will ever desire is just beyond your comfort zone. Jim Rohn said that the beauty of goals is not so much in achieving them, but enticing you to become who you need to be in order to reach and achieve those goals. Relentless pursuit of goals is the catalyst to meaningful achievement. The question then is, what are you becoming? This enables you to reach within, tap into your own resourcefulness to see what is available, recognising what external resources are required in order to fulfil a particular desire.

This calls for acquiring a new skills set to know how to communicate your needs and negotiate with others in order to get the tools you need to achieve those goals. It calls for a new mindset to know within yourself that you can do it, and if others can, so can you. We will delve more deeply into this in a later chapter.

3) USE DEADLINES AS LIFELINES - TAKE MASSIVE ACTION

A deadline creates results, crystalises thinking and increases motivation. There is a sense of urgency and sharpness of thinking that enables things to happen as a result of this.

One way of creating deadlines is by dividing the year into quarters as they do in the world of finance, then set goals with strategies of how to achieve them according to completion dates. Each quarter, sit down to assess and evaluate them, make adjustments, tick off and celebrate achievements to give yourself momentum to set bigger goals which enable you to stretch beyond your comfort zone.

So for example, you may want a full garden manicure by end of first quarter. This allows you to factor in the resources necessary in terms of time, money and manpower before embarking on this, as well as take into consideration the weather elements that affect the execution of the project. This also ensures that you're not just waiting for the new year to make resolutions that don't work. It helps keep momentum going too because part of the strategies that lead up to the quarterly assessment, are weekly and daily action steps that ultimately lead to the goal completion

A deadline creates results, crystalizes thinking and increases motivation. There is a sense of urgency and sharpness of thinking that enables things to happen

Decide exactly what you want in each area from the wheel of life.

Imagine that there are no limitations on what you can be, do or have. Imagine that neither time nor money were a hindrance to your goal accomplishments. What would a picture of perfection look like in each area? Divide goals into short, medium and long term deadlines, encompassing 5/10/50/100/200 year plans.

This forces your subconscious mind to drive you, consciously and unconsciously toward achieving your goal on schedule. For bigger goals, set sub-deadlines.

If for whatever reason you don't achieve your goal by the deadline, simply set a new deadline. All things are possible; there are no unreasonable goals, only unreasonable deadlines. Identify and pre-empt any obstacles that you may have to overcome to achieve your goal. Evaluate situations and take decisive action. You cannot change what you will not confront, and progress is a risk-taking exercise. Consistency is key, as it is the one word that separates those who reach their goals from those who fall short.

On the subject of resolutions, the reason they don't actually work is because they are usually based on negatives rather than positives. For instance, the top two common ones are: I want to stop smoking or I want to lose weight. These usually are thrown out the window come January the 14th when 'reality' kicks in. Due to the nature of the goal being based on a negative, it removes the element of drive and motivation, whereas a goal of adopting a healthier lifestyle is more likely attainable due to its positive intent. Resolutions are also somewhat based on peer pressure and just jumping in with what the crowd assumes, because 'everyone' is doing it.

When goals are self-motivated, they have greater meaning. Now because a resolution is not an internal decision with a strong 'why' factor, it quickly looses its zeal and momentum, along with the crowd psychology of 'giving up those resolutions' that the rest of them adopt.

Once you set a deadline, take massive action toward your goal because action is the bridge between thought and reality. An action plan is going beyond knowing what you need to do - which is information - to getting it done. A good idea implemented today is better than a perfect idea to be done tomorrow. Why? Because tomorrow never comes – it's an illusion. A deadline becomes a lifeline because pressure begins to mount as the set time becomes imminent, causing you to somehow find the resources to execute the goal on time. This is the same psychology that you would experience when you know an exam or assignment is due.

I had the goal of living a debt free life. During my years at university, I accumulated a huge amount of 'five-figure' debt. This was in the form of loans, credit cards, store cards and car payments - typical student life, or 'normal', as it is perceived. I had to stop ignoring the fact that if I didn't do anything about this debt, it would continue to accrue and spiral out of control. So I took responsibility and gave myself a year to come out of debt. Firstly I made a list of all my creditors and wrote down the exact amounts and interest figures alongside this. I got a copy of my credit report, in order to have an understanding of where I was.

Next was to research all I could about debt management and alleviation, through studying the lives of those that have come out of it. A highly recommended Personal Finance Expert is Dave Ramsey, who has easy to follow practical steps and the psychology to back up his theories. Following his recommendations, I quickly gathered an emergency fund to keep my head above the water while embarking on crossing this river of debt. Then, using the "Debt Snowball" method, listed my debts from smallest to largest, and attacked the smallest one with a vengeance, while paying the minimum payments on the rest. This gave enough momentum and zeal to face the next one, having attained the thrill from accomplishing a baby step. So when one was finished, I used the payment amount from the previous debt, and used it to attack the next debt, and so on.

Nine months on, and I was out of debt! It took, discipline, focus, consistency, persistence and relentless determination in order to stay the course and finish well. Now, it was not easy at all, being mocked, scorned, jested and belittled from especially close relations about how broke I was looking during that time and how evident it was that I was going through financial hardship. Nevertheless, I had made up my mind that despite all, I would do what it takes to come out of that dark place. It took nine gruesome months to deliver the baby of financial freedom and it was not

Discipline is the bridge between setting goals and accomplishing them.

without the typical symptoms of retching, contractions, pain, swellings, and everything else that goes with pregnancy. Today, from the land of freedom, I look over and wonder how quickly the comments over my financial predicament have vanished and instead begun to reflect their very own lives! In sharing my experience and strategies, I hope to help liberate as many as are willing to embrace the principles, including those that didn't necessarily support me when I set out in pursuit of my goal to be debt free. To top it all up, I beat my own deadline of accomplishing this goal in 12 months, and managed to cross the finish line in nine months instead.

Set goals with concrete deadlines to achieve them. Whether you are laughed at, mocked or jested about by others, realise that your life is in your hands. Happiness in your life is dependent on you and not from anyone outside. Therefore, take full ownership and responsibility of your life. Let the locus of control be within you.

4) BE "ECO-FRIENDLY"; RECYCLE GOALS

Constantly evaluate and adjust your goals according to your progress, then finally reward yourself and celebrate your achievements. The behaviour you reward is the behaviour you will repeat. While you are still high in triumph and momentum, set new, bolder and bigger goals beyond your wildest imagination. Eventually you come to realise that goals are a continuous cycle with strategies that you can recycle - an incessant process of reinvention, reassessment and re-setting.

It's like in school where you had weekly tests to assess whether you had understood what you had been taught throughout the week. This was a form of constant evaluation. You would then have half term tests and then end of term tests in order to go on to the next level. This helped you to grow in understanding and mastery of certain subjects. In the same way, this constant evaluation becomes a yardstick to measure progress towards a desired goal. You begin to find the answers to certain questions like: What is working or not working? What needs to be increased or decreased? What can be tweaked to make it work?

This becomes important because sometimes when a goal is made, circumstances and conditions of achieving the goal may differ from when the goal was first set. For instance, one may desire to do a Masters in Business Administration (MBA) within two years, get started, but then move to another country for whatever reason, and so this may stall the progress or mean starting all over again. In some cases, people give up at this point, saying maybe I was not meant to do it. A goal is a goal and must be pursued at all costs, This should be no excuse. There are so many ways of tweaking a goal to make it work and in this case they could complete their studies online as one way of bypassing this challenge..

Upon completion and achievement of those goals, celebrate yourself. Reward yourself along the way, to keep it interesting. Tony Robins highlights that as human beings, we tend to make decisions to move either away from pain, or towards pleasure. The reward and celebratory factor then pulls you and keeps you in the game to make it happen. In the frenzy of celebration, set new goals immediately, so that it becomes a cycle of success and achievement and it ultimately elevates you to become an unstoppable force that can achieve anything you put your heart and mind to. This enables growth to take place in which you come to a place where you appreciate yourself more, respect yourself, and gain the respect and admiration of others. Ultimately what you create is a lifestyle of goal setting, goal getting, goal achieving, and enjoying the journey as you go along. As the saying goes, life is a journey and not a destination. You realise also that the proverbial 'Promised Land' of goals is not a place you 'go to', but rather you 'grow to'.

You can't hit a target that you can't see, therefore your attention should be focused on an achievement. The starting point of great success is when you sit down and decide exactly what you really want, in every area of your life. Then you sketch a plan to make it happen. There have been countless studies done comparing people who took the time to set goals and those who did not. 97% of those who set their goals and stayed focused on those goals, achieved their objectives. They won. And those who had no particular goal came up far short.

The most remarkable thing about setting and focusing on goals is that it works on every facet of life! When business owners set goals, their odds of becoming more profitable skyrocket. When athletes set goals, they invariably get stronger, faster, and better. People get wealthier, healthier, more spiritually connected, and more popular with friends and family. Setting your goals and referring to them daily and weekly just takes a little time, a pen, and some paper. Many prominent business people start their day with either a written or a mental to-do list. If you were to take away their to-do lists, many of them would be lost .Yet, as much as many of us rely on our daily or weekly to-do lists, only about 5% of us take the time to regularly shape our own future by setting goals.

SUMMARY

When you decide to live your life on purpose, setting goals shows that you are ready to step into the next version of you. Don't be afraid. Stop being scared to make a mistake, and stop playing small. Every success has a trail of failures behind it, and every failure is leading towards success. As John C. Maxwell puts it, 'Fail Forward'. Aim higher, beyond your comfort zone. You don't need to wait for permission - give yourself permission to blossom, shine, arise, glow, grow, flourish, be! Get rid of your excuses, you are not a victim of your past. Someone else's opinion of you does not have to become your reality. You define what success means to you personally, not what society, parents, teachers, family, peers, media thinks, but what success is to You.

REFLECTION POINTS:

Ask yourself provocative questions to help you think. For example, why aren't you already at your goal? This will help you identify existing limitations that you may have, and thereby indicate the type of resources required to overcome those limitations. You may want to start a business and don't know how to start or what to start. This will immediately indicate a skill or knowledge gap. You can then start to close and fill in that gap by taking a course in business studies, researching into a particular business, or finding a mentor to teach you how that business system operates.

What are the 10 main reasons why you want to accomplish these goals, or why you will not quit at any costs? Decide right now.

Do a stock-check and introspection. Ask yourself for example, What resources do I have available to me? What resources do I require? What are my strengths? Who has those resources and how can I access them? What are my threats concerning each area of my life? The answers lie within; draw them out, or solicit help from a mentor/coach to help bring them out of you, such as someone who has been where you are, or where you want to go. Save on time, shorten your own learning curve, avoid unnecessary obstacles and frustrations and don't try to re-invent the wheel.

ACTION POINTS:

Download the wheel of life from the internet on
www.wheeloflifeinteractive.com and complete it.
See what areas of your life need a balance and start
to work on these.

Set three top BHAG goals which you would like to
accomplish in each area, writing them down in deadline categories of short, medium and long term goals.

Make an assessment of your current resources and
those needed to accomplish that goal. Put your reasons next to your goals as a reminder and motivator.
Take action immediately on the easiest step. Set quarterly reviews of all goals and make it a reward session
as well to look forward to. Once completed, celebrate and set new, higher stretching goals again.

'We are relational beings, created for con- nection and no man is an island.'

SUCCESS
GRAVITY

CHAPTER 2

Relationships

1)   FRIEND OR FOE: WHAT ARE YOU TO YOU?

Strong individuals make strong families, which in turn make strong communities, organisations, workforces and ultimately strong nations around the world. It all starts with the individual.

Loving yourself builds your confidence, self-esteem, and courage to make choices that lead to success! Loving others helps you love yourself. Loving yourself helps you love others.

The relationship you have within yourself determines how you relate to others too. Be your best friend and cheerleader. Self-awareness begins the healthy relationships process. If you are whole within yourself, and balanced in the way you relate with yourself, then this can foster strong bonds with other people on the outside. You can only give what you yourself have. It is important to lay down this foundation in order for you to understand that ultimately the onus is on you to decide how relationships go.

There is a great model for self-awareness called the Johari window, formulated by Joseph Luft and Harrington Ingram in 1954, It is a diagram that is divided into four quadrants. The first is the area known to yourself and others - Open Area; then there is the area known to self and hidden from others - Hidden Area; next is the side of yourself known by others and unknown to you - Blind area, and finally, the side of yourself that is unknown to you or others - Unknown area. I recently did an experiment with a group of friends in order to discover more about how others see us in comparison to how we see ourselves. Each of us went round the group, taking it in turns to be in the 'spotlight' to let the others evaluate us and give us feedback on the way they see us. This was done in a spirit of love, growth and maturity.

If you are whole within yourself, and balanced in the way you relate with yourself, then this can foster strong bonds with other people on the outside.

We highlighted the good and also recommended areas of growth, being careful in language and articulation to make it a useful exercise for all of us. Indeed, it was a very productive, eye opening session that, interestingly enough, also reflected the different filters that people use in order to come to conclusions or opinions about others. I must say though, that this experiment may produce very different results in different settings. For example, in a work scenario or family setting, depending on the existing dynamics, it may be taken as an opportunity to gripe and complain about an individual and ultimately sabotage, ruin reputations and assassinate the characters of individuals. In our case however, the bonds and dynamics between us are quite healthy. We were all enlightened to discover themes of good traits being revealed to us that we had not observed about ourselves prior to this exercise.

Now you may have gone through a traumatic period in your life that caused you to hate yourself. You may have been violated and this was beyond your own control and I acknowledge that. Some people have endured rape, physical and verbal abuse, rejection, isolation, belittlement, or told to their face that they would never amount to anything, leading to possible self-doubt, loss of self-esteem and self hate. You can't unscramble those eggs. The question is, what are you going to do about it? You can take back your power in changing the meaning you attach to events and know that you are not an event, you are a whole person. You are no longer a victim, but now a victor because you went through all that and are still standing! Change the interpretation of meaning you attach to the event. The key is also in recognising that someone else's opinion of you does not have to become your reality. You can create your own reality. You are not a product of your experiences or your past. You are who you were created to be and who you choose to become.

We are all creative beings, endowed with seeds of greatness, and can choose to tap into these in-built resources within us for success. In his book 'Born to Win', Zig Ziglar states: "You are born to win, designed for accomplishment, engineered for success, crafted for championship, and created to conquer". Choosing to ride on this wave of positive energy ensures access to success in life and how you relate to yourself. You have to believe you can do it. Henry Ford said: "The man who thinks he can and the man who thinks he can't are both right. Which one are you?" Les Brown puts it this way: "If there is no enemy within, the enemy outside can do us no harm". So, love on yourself - be good with you and be good to you.

Loving yourself builds your confidence, self-esteem, and courage to make choices that lead to success

Get a healthy perspective of yourself and do the things you love. Be good to yourself and treat yourself right. In so doing, you teach others how to treat you. Set the pace, set the standard. Respect yourself, find out about yourself, get excited about spending time with you. In time you find that you begin to exude that energy where others gravitate towards you because you become a magnet rather than a repellent. Love on yourself, spoil yourself; if you can't stand being alone, how can you expect others to stand being around you? George Bernard Shaw asserted: "Life is not about finding yourself; life is about creating yourself".

2)   FELLOWS, FOES, FAMILY, FRIENDS - THE SURVIVAL TOOL KIT

Your associations are a crucial part of your success. We are relational beings, created for connection and no man is an island. Work on building good relationships with others starting with your immediate circles of influence: friends; family; fellow workers; members of a group you belong to; coaches; mentors; protégés; bosses; peers; subordinates; contractors, and assistants.

Building successful relationships is about finding common ground or creating rapport with the people you relate to. This is what will form a bridge through which experiences can be shared and value can be exchanged.

Assessing the people around you and what their function serves in your life is very crucial, as some people are there for a REASON, a SEASON or a LIFE-TIME. The metaphor of a tree helps shed light on this principle. The leaves represent those that come into your life for a reason. They show up with you when you are successful and provide some shade during the summer, but when the wind blows, they are very shaky and come 'winter time' in your life, they are no longer a part of it. They 'leave' just like their name implies. Some leaves come in the form of peers or can even disguise themselves as friends.

Next are the branches; these are firmer in giving you structure and are there much longer, but under pressure, they can break on you as well. These are the people who are around for a certain season in your life, whether long or short. An example of branches would be co-workers or group associates. Lastly are the roots. These are the people that don't need to claim responsibility for your success as they are hidden underground. However, they are responsible for helping you stay firm and rooted, providing water and nourishment for every season of your life. They are there for the long haul, the lifetime people. Examples of roots would be mentors and coaches.

I heard a sermon preached by Bishop T.D Jakes on relationships and this was revolutionary, too good not to share with you: In summary, he reiterated that you cannot be limited to only hang around people who think, act, talk, vote or dress like you. That is too narrow and one-dimensional. You have to get out of the box and expose yourself to a wider scope of experiences, opinions and perspectives in order to grow and walk in your destiny. There are therefore three basic types of people you will come across in your life: Confidants, Constituents and Comrades. Confidants are those that love you unconditionally and are into You, whether you are up or down, right or wrong. There are very few of them and they are in it for the long haul. An example is a mentor - you can share anything with them and they are not afraid to tell you when you are wrong.

Constituents are not into you, but they are for what you are for. As long as you are for what they are for, they will walk and work with you, but don't be mistaken that they are for you. If they meet somebody else that will further their agenda, they will leave you because they were never for you to begin with. Never mistake a Constituent for a confidant because to them, it's all about the cause that you represent.

Building successful relationships is about finding common ground or creating rapport with the people you relate to.

Then lastly, there are comrades. These are not for you or for what you are for; they are just against what you are against. They will team up with you to help fight a greater enemy. Don't be confused by their association, they will only be with you until the victory is accomplished. They are like scaffolding - they come into your life only to fulfill a purpose, and when the purpose is achieved, the scaffolding is removed. Don't be upset either when they are gone, because the building still stands and remains after the scaffolding is removed. Expect the constituents and the comrades to leave after a while, but the confidant will always be there. The other two may not react to your dream the same way you may expect them to, but don't be upset - just be careful then who you tell your dream to. Realise also that you don't succeed alone. What a powerful analogy on relationships!

There will always be helpers of destiny sent along to aid you on the path as you go through different levels in your life. Life is lived in levels and arrived at in stages and I believe each stage of the way is usually defined by the new relationships that enter your life. Conventional wisdom has it that 'Fate controls who walks into your life, but you decide who you let walk out, who you let stay, and who you refuse to let go'. Therefore, I say, know which bridges to build, and which ones to burn.

It is important, however, to note that foes can be propellants of destiny as well, meaning at times an enemy can actually help you more than a friend does. Enemies can tell you the truth and 'harsh reality' you need to hear, while friends can sometimes flatter you to obscurity. Enemies can be used as sandpaper to smoothen and polish any rough edges you have around you.

Still on the contrary, some people are just energy drainers; they may be in the boat with you, but they are either rowing in the opposite direction, or creating holes in your boat so that it eventually sinks or goes nowhere. These are time wasters and are not deserving of your attention.

I operated a small-scale import and export retail business before, and I quickly got to learn the difference in language and behaviour between a serious buyer and a time waster. Often, the time wasters would look at what I had to sell, and try to devalue the merchandise in order to negotiate a ridiculous offer. Needless to say, they would have none of my business. On the other hand, the serious buyers would appreciate the value of my merchandise and negotiate terms of payment if need be. I would then negotiate an even better bargain for quicker clearance of balance, or offer incentives and extras. Soon all this became an interesting psychological 'game' to me, where I was able to tell the difference between the time waters and the serious ones as soon as they opened their mouth or approached me. I would immediately know whether I would want to do business with them or not.

These principles are applicable in life relationships as well. Now this is not about judging people, but about discerning intent from the beginning, and not ignoring the warning signs. In addition to this, it is important to note that healthy relationships are also about forgiving mistakes and allowing others to be their true authentic self. This involves transparency and boundary setting. Honouring boundaries in personal relationships is parallel to honouring terms and conditions in business relationships.

3) YOUR NETWORK DETERMINES YOUR NET WORTH

According to studies done in 1929 by Frigyes Karinthy, it truly is a small world. His Theory of Six Degrees contends that, because we are all linked by chains of associations, you are just six people away from everyone else in the world. This is the concept from which the social media platform LinkedIn emerged. Of late, the online world in social media has cut this figure down to 4 degrees of separation. There are numerous stories and testimonials we hear about how people got a breakthrough in life or business through a connection or referral. I have been able to move from a place of being stuck, to unstoppable, through the help of a brilliant coach that I got to know through a motivational speaker that spoke at my church. In writing this book for instance, I faced a lot of blocks and challenges and would not have been able to overcome these obstacles without his input. He helped pull out of me what was in me already. I got to realise that I did not need to wait for further external resources as I had done my training on book writing, read many books, and had enough knowledge and experience in me to share with the world and help change someone else's life by doing so.

I got over excuses and procrastination and also kicked out the fear of success that was slowly beginning to creep in. I was also getting stuck psychologically in that the reward for 'playing small' and staying in my comfort zone ensured that I would not have to take the big responsibility that comes with success and being published. He helped me realise that I could be playing a bigger game and I owed it to the people I wanted to serve, to myself as well as to my Creator. So I eventually took the plunge, and the book is now here in your hands today. It took a coach, like a midwife, to help birth and bring out of me what I had inside me already. It is good to keep company with people that have the same goals as you.

Sometimes you need an outside perspective to take a look at it from another angle in order to get the full picture, because after all, you can't see the picture when you are in the frame.

You need others in your life to keep reminding you of your greatness, to be cheerleaders when you need it and to give you a swift kick in the backside as the situation demands. I am so grateful for those types of people who have been in my life. Some of them, I paid (coaches and teachers) while others were paying me (bosses and executives). Some were mentors who I've met along the way, and others were people long gone from my life. Some will never leave my life, but very few just 'came' to me. I was proactive in developing the relationships and letting them know what I needed. They challenged me to think differently, to do things that were uncomfortable so that I could get what I said I wanted. To get over myself, my ego and my prideful attitude to become a true student who is open to learning the hard lessons of life. I hear many people say they long for someone like that in their corner, who will refuse to let them settle for less than their best. If that's you, you must take the necessary steps to forge that level of rapport.

I was also getting stuck psychologically, in that the reward for 'playing small' and staying in my comfort zone ensured that I would not have to take the big responsibility that comes with success

4)   FROM COMPETITION TO COLLABORATION

Since 2003, the audience has shifted from a 'Me' mindset to a 'We' mindset, with increased intensity. Values of community, social impact, relationships and authenticity are rapidly taking over from the old values of individualism, personal expression and "what's in it for me?" If you don't adapt your communications style to tap into the new 'We' mindset, you'll see a gradual decline as your marketing goes stale and people stop responding to your calls to action. To keep your finger on the pulse of today's marketplace it is important to make the necessary paradigm shift.

Over the last few years, the notion of collaborative consumption has increasingly become widely accepted by individuals. This is a system whereby products or services required are shared on a customer-to-customer basis. People with similar needs or interests, band together to share and exchange products and services. Users pay for the benefit of using a product without needing to own the product outright. So for instance, if you own a car that you hardly use, you can rent it out for a day or a week to someone who doesn't necessarily want to own a car, but needs it for a short period of time. That way it becomes a win-win situation. More examples include: taxi shares, home help sharing, shared rental space in business, crowd funding, bike sharing, outsourcing, virtual currency, and the list is endless.

A collaboration mindset helps pull you towards the right circle of interest. You start to draw towards like-minded people and gravitate towards where you are tolerated. This is why it is important to form masterminds as they enable the group to pull and pool mental resources together for a common success goal. By cooperating with your competitors, as they are in the same field already, you can ride on each other's back. That is the beauty of affiliation and syndication.

To help you maintain focus, join mastermind groups with like-minded people that will challenge you to grow as you also simultaneously add value to the group. Attend networking seminars: these are places where you can actually get joint venture partnerships to team up with others for a common success goal. Another form of connection especially in the world of online business is becoming an affiliate. This is about marketing someone else's business, product or service to an audience in return for a percentage of any sales successfully transacted through your marketing. Some people actually choose this as a solo career, and become an online affiliate marketer - a very lucrative industry if conducted right. I find that this breaks barriers in competition as one can actually partner with a competitor in order to get ahead in their own business as well through making referrals. However, this has to be done strategically, ethically and intelligently.

I host foreign exchange students and guests in my home and am always fascinated by the wealth of knowledge they bring. The exposure to different cultures and experiences has so enriched my life that my horizon for decision-making has been extended. I am offered a wider range of 'lenses' and perspectives to look through different aspects of life, removing any previous limitations of one-dimensional thinking. In exchange for that, they get a warm, inexpensive friendly home with a 'British Cultural' feel to it, instead of some impersonal, expensive hotel where the service may not necessarily meet their particular needs or standards.

Besides enhancing relationship skills, what I particularly relish is the connectivity after the period of hosting. I get a variety of invites and contacts from many different countries and hence I always say I have a home in any part of the world. Now, of course, not all my guests have compatible characters with mine. However, I have become richer by way of knowing them and they have been enriched as well in return. Suffice it to say that in as much as they save on tourist accommodation, it is a nice steady stream of passive income for me.

I now network with other hosts in the area and we help each other manage guests and make referrals amongst ourselves when overbooked, instead of competing and fighting for guests. Collaboration has really become the new vehicle in order to get ahead in life.

SUMMARY

Whether you choose a mentor, a coach, an executive at your company or someone you admire in your industry, here are some tips to maximise the relationship:

1. Be clear about your goals and what you want to achieve.

2. Identify the traits and characteristics that make the person a good mentor for you - and tell them.

3. Agree on the formality or informality of communication. Will you have regular scheduled meetings or will you contact them periodically when you need specific advice?

4. Decide how you'll measure whether the mentorship is working.

5. Is the relationship about information, guidance and advice or about connections and introductions?

6. Be respectful of their time.

7. Always follow through on YOUR commitments to your mentor. Do what you say you are going to do. And when you do develop that type of relationship, and you have a mentor just as committed to your call to greatness as you say you are, you have to be willing to stay in the game.

REFLECTION POINTS:

Using the SWOT model again, recognise and acknowledge your strengths whilst working on improving the weaknesses. Think about making strategic alliances with someone who is strong in your weak areas. Study and take advantage of your opportunities and confront your threats to eliminate them. You may for example be well articulated in strength, while your weakness is being a bad listener. Your opportunities would lie in enhancing your communication skills by going on personal development or communication course. You would then need to look out for threats in the form of condescending voices in your head or past experiences resurfacing.

Have a healthy outlook on life, realising that you don't need permission or validation from anyone to go after the life of your dreams. You come to a place where you give yourself permission to get grounded success.

R

ACTION POINTS:

To get a better understanding of yourself and others, download the DISC profile from the Discovery Report Website and fill it in. DISC represents for four distinct character traits that individuals possess (Dominant; Influential; Steady, and Contemplating). This is one of the frequently used tools that indicate the most prevalent character traits in individuals.

The profile gives you an indication of the strengths and blind-spots of that particular character trait, together with recommendations of what variations blend well together and what to avoid. In a work setting, it is useful to know the personality types of your co-workers in order to relate to them better. Many organisations and corporations use this profile in interview settings when recruiting for jobs.

Carry out the 'Johari Window' exercise with friends in order to increase self-awareness and help establish healthier relationships.

Take time to consciously discern the type of people that walk into your life. Discover who deserves the investment of your time and simultaneously spot and eliminate the time waters. Now, you cannot always tell how a connection in life or business will go, but past episodes will set off alarm bells for attention when needed. This is where mentors come in and teach you what to avoid ahead of time. Find a mentor if you don't have one already. They will shorten the learning curve for you in helping you attain Grounded Success.

'Our deepest fear
is not that we
are inadequate.
Our deepest fear
is that we are
powerful beyond
measure.'

SUCCESS
GRAVITY

CHAPTER 3

Attitude

Attitude is a sum total of your Thoughts, Personal Philosophy, Beliefs, Values and Behaviour. Most success in life and business is usually about how you think, feel and behave, rather than the tools and resources at hand. That is why it is now more important to work on your Emotional Intelligence and Emotional Quotient, as opposed to just Intelligence Quotient. Don't count yourself out just because society has counted you out. You are never too old, too dark or too young, and it does not matter what colour, creed or societal background you are. You are only as old and as poor as you think.

In order to illustrate this key, I will share a full quote from Charles Swindoll:

"The longer I live, the more I realise the impact of attitude on life. Attitude to me is more than facts. It is more important than the past, an education, than money, than circumstances, than failure, than success, than what others think or say or do. It is more important than appearance, giftedness or skill. It will make or break a company, a church, a home. The remarkable thing is we have a choice every-day regarding the attitude we will embrace for that day. We cannot change our past... we cannot change the fact that people will act a certain way. We cannot change the inevitable. The only thing we can do is play on the string we have, and that is our attitude... I am convinced that life is 10% what happens to me and 90% how I react to it. And so it is with you... we are in charge of our attitudes."

I)   ATTITUDE DETERMINES AITITUDE

Attitude portrays filters of circumstance - how you see, perceive and interpret everything. What you look at may not be what you see. Your frame of mind determines the way you process what is input with-in you. So firstly, it's the acquiring of information (Input), then your processing (attitude filter), and finally the outcome as a result of that information filter (output). What becomes crucial then, is to have a healthy processing filter in order to enjoy Grounded Success.

Stop being idle and don't think too much or you'll cre-ate a problem that wasn't even there in the first place. The Bible says "The race is not to the swift, nor the battle to the strong, nor bread to the wise, but time and chance happen to all". I want to submit to you that you can create your chance and opportunities if you sense that you have missed them. Don't wait for them to come always. Prepare ahead of time, and surely when opportunity meets preparation, grounded success becomes inevitable.

If you think you can, you can. Attitude consists of beliefs and values that shape your thought process, habits, actions, and ultimately your destiny. Attitude also forms character, as you eventually become what you believe. What you believe determines how far you can go. It was Henry Ford who said, "The man who thinks he can and he who thinks he cannot are both correct".

A famous quote from Marianne Williamson from her book, A Return to Love, summarises it this way: "Our deepest fear is not that we are inadequate. Our deepest fear is that we are powerful beyond measure. It is our light, not our darkness that most frightens us. We ask ourselves, "Who am I to be brilliant, gorgeous, talented, and fabulous?" Actually who are you not to be? You are a child of God. Your playing small does not serve the world. There is nothing enlightened about shrinking so that people won't feel insecure around you. We are all meant to shine as children do. Its not just in some of us, it's in everyone. And as we let our own light shine, we unconsciously give other people permission to do the same. As we are liberated from our own fear, our presence automatically liberates others".

Your attitude therefore determines your altitude, so how you think determines how far or how high you can go to achieve your goals.

As Dale Carnegie asserts, 'Happiness doesn't depend on who you are or what you have; it depends solely on what you think'. What then becomes important is what you feed your mind and what you expose yourself to.

> Happiness doesn't depend on who you are or what you have; it depends solely on what you think.

Attitude is also behaviour and demeanour. When one is going for an interview for instance, attitude becomes a huge deciding factor between two people with similar backgrounds and qualifications. The usual million dollar question the interviewers want to know is what you can bring to the company. Now if you have not done your research on the company, it surfaces as an attitude of negligence, selfishness, lack of preparation and lack of diligence. It screams out, "I don't care!" All this does not serve you or the company in the long run. On the other hand, responding with a bit of statistics about the company, its competitors, its strengths and weaknesses, is more likely to demonstrate an attitude of care and ownership of aspired position. You are therefore more likely to be hired on the spot. It pays to go that extra mile beyond your expected duties and responsibilities. Paula Abdul says, "There are no traffic jams beyond the extra mile". So true, and this is also about what you do when no one is watching, when there is no reward for doing it.

I believe we all have the capacity to craft out the life of our dreams and have the guts to go after it, doing whatever it takes - within moral and ethical limits - to get there.

2)   YOUR PAST IS PAST: HARVEST THE LESSONS

Now as a child, you may not have had the choice to shape your attitude, as it was your surroundings and environmental culture that conditioned your beliefs, values and norms. You cannot unscramble those eggs. However, as an adult, it's important to know that you can choose your own beliefs. Those notions that no longer serve you or your purpose, you now have the power to discard them. I will give you a personal example. I was born into a culture that places emphasis on recognition of positional authority. This means that if you are the first born, your younger siblings succumb to your authority and decisions, and positional power loses its potency as you go down the line. So being the last born of six children meant that I was last in absolutely everything!

It meant that I was last to dish the food, last to bath, which was ok on a school day, but on a Sunday when we were all rushing to go to church, all I would hear was: "Hurry up, hurry up, you are delaying the others!" But I didn't have enough time as the others to prepare. Oh, life always seemed unfair as the last born child. Moreover, being lastborn meant that I was last to speak, if at all I was "allowed" to speak because most conversations were for the "grown ups". Everything seemed to be just about the grown ups. If I heard it once, I heard it a thousand times: the grown ups, the grown ups! I couldn't wait to grow up.

So I took this mindset to school, that I was last in everything. People thought that I was quiet because I always waited for 'permission' to speak. You might be able to relate with this scenario: You are all in class, and the teacher asks a question, and you whisper out the answer, then somebody with a louder voice than you shouts out the answer and gets the credit for it! Well that was my story. That would annoy me so much, and I lost many a medal along the way because of that. I blamed myself because I knew I could have shouted louder, but something in me would just assure me that 'it was ok' and 'I deserved this'.

There was one particular day I remember a prize was to be given - the 'badge of the week' - to the person who got the answer correct first and I had the opportunity to make my parents proud that week. So as usual, I whispered out the answer, and my classmate Renate shouted out the answer and got the prize instead of me! I was so devastated, and what is worse is that those around me heard me say out the answer, and still, none of them stood up for me. Yet still, something in me said 'you deserve this'. Another scenario was during the swimming gala. I was an excellent swimmer at school, so on this day during the competitions, I could hear my house team cheering for me and shouting out my name. So as I got to the end, I heard the slogans and could see them stumping their feet in excitement.

So I looked up, and saw that I was about to beat the defending champion, and for some reason, I slowed down...and missed out on the gold! Man! I was extremely devastated and later on when I sat down to analyse all this I realised that I had gone into 'self sabotage'. I had told myself that I was last in everything, remember? So how could I have possibly taken up the title of swimming champion? How could I possibly wear the 'badge for the week?' Who was I to do that and be that?

Those notions that no longer serve you or your purpose, you now have the power to discard them.

My attitude and belief had been shaped up by culture and that had become a hindrance to my success on any level. That all changed in junior high school when one day I got invited to a youth camp by my friend for the weekend. On the first night, they told us all to stand up in front of everyone and talk about ourselves, our family backgrounds, and share our hopes and dreams. What they specifically told us that night was that none of us would go to bed, until every last one of us had got up to speak. Now this wasn't a cruel exercise; it was done in order to help us break barriers in fear, shyness and intimidation, as well as build confidence in communication, rapport and self-esteem.

When I got up to speak that night, I couldn't believe that no one interrupted me; they were all attentive and engaged in what I had to say. They smiled and nodded and were interested in what I, the last one, was saying? When I realised this, I grew wings and projected my voice to the back of the room so loudly and for the first time, I heard how beautiful my voice was! I stood tall and allowed confidence to well up on the inside of me, and from then on, there was no turning back. I became unstoppable! I went back home and went back to school with renewed confidence, knowing that what I had to say was important and was worth others listening to. That experience forever changed my life. So it took someone holding my hand, to know that I too could speak up. That helped shape my attitude as I could now look at my life from a space and a mindset of a victor, rather than a victim.

I had to learn to let go of what was no longer serving me. The happiest of people don't necessarily have the best of everything; they just make the most of everything that comes their way. The brightest future will always be based on a forgotten past. You can't go forward in life until you let go of past failure and heartaches. It's like a monkey swinging on a tree. In order for it to get to another branch, it has to let go of the one it is currently holding. Then and only then can it swing forward. In the same way, to move in and enjoy life, we must let go of what no longer serves us.

3)   BATTLEFIELD OF THE MIND

Where the mind goes, the man follows. You gravitate towards your most dominant thoughts. Therefore fill your mind with what you want to see. Results follow actions, which in turn follow thoughts, and thoughts are attitude. Think positive and positive will happen, and the contrary is true. The scriptures say: "As a man thinks in his heart, so is he".

My experiences and change in mental scope had a ripple effect on my decision-making and thought processing. Having a healthy outlook on myself also helped me understand and embrace all my other experiences. Trying and failing on different attempts at business, for example, does not make you a failure.

It is said that you fail your way to success. The pathway to success is littered with failure, and failure is an event and not a person. Changing the meaning you attach to events gives empowerment. In other words, the difference between success and failure could just be a paradigm shift.

There are three ways in which you can alter the concept of failure in your mind. Firstly, associate failure with Courage. This is where you begin to view the failure process as a series of events that reflect boldness, stepping out of the comfort zone and trying out something new. Secondly, associate failure with Progress. The lessons learnt are always valuable to keep as you take more steps towards your desired goal; fail forward. It is somewhat a paradox that failure can actually be a blessing because rather than it being the opposite of success, it is in fact the pathway that leads you there.

I came up with an acronym for the word FAIL, and it simply stands for: Find Another Important Lesson. Either way, you win, as you learn what not to do the next time. Failure is not final. Failure is feedback and feedback is the food of Champions!

Lastly, associate failure with honour. It is commendable to at least try something, rather than sit back, fold your arms and moan that things never work for you. After all they don't erect statues for cowards, but in honour of heroes who fought their way through failure until they overcame. A prize is awarded for participating and for winning, not for watching.

What would have happened if Thomas Edison gave up just before the 10,000th attempt? None of today's modern necessities, things we often take for granted, would have come into existence. His own conclusions were: "I have not failed, I have just found 10,000 ways that won't work". You've got to love that!

It may be that you realise you have a "gap" in knowledge, skills or resources that needs to be filled. When my associate and I first opened up our dental practice, we had all the right knowledge and skills for the job, delivering high quality dentistry by any standards. However, there was a lack of knowledge of how business systems run. The game had changed and the rules for the old game could no longer apply. Being excellent in skill doesn't automatically translate to being excellent in business even of the same industry. We soon learned this, as we decided to move on after two years of running the practice. Needless to say also, we had set up the practice at the dawn of the economic recession, which stacked more odds against us.

I am convinced that life is 10% what happens to me and 90% how I react to it. And so it is with you... we are in charge of our attitudes.

However, I decided to go back to school and learn exactly how business systems operate. This was knowledge that I would later use, not only in dentistry, but in virtually any business that I will encounter along life's path. So I did my Postgraduate in Management studies, covering all the essentials of business in Marketing, Human Resources, Finance and Information Technology. I proudly graduated with a distinction. I don't say this to impress you, but to impress upon you that failure in one venture can actually open bigger doors in the future if you decide to pick yourself up and embrace the lessons learned.

Whereas one might look at the scenario and call me a failure, I looked at it as courage to boldly open up a dental practice in the UK, and also as progress, since I am wiser now in my business dealings. I have also acquired knowledge in operating different business systems. Lastly, it is an honourable thing for you to at least attempt something rather than 'play it safe', sit back, fold your arms and not even try. Vince Lombardi is quoted as saying: "But I firmly believe that any man's finest hour - his greatest fulfilment to all he holds dear - is that moment when he has worked his heart out in a good cause and lies exhausted on the field of battle, victorious". So whatever it is you want to achieve in life, do it anyway, even if it means doing it afraid.

Another new mind alteration that empowered me was that of moving from perfectionism to excellence. Perfectionism stunts progress, and also works hand in hand with procrastination as you wait for all conditions to be perfect before attempting. My favourite book says 'he who observes the wind will never plough'. It leaves no room for failure and growth. Perfectionism brings frustration, and fosters a quitting attitude. On the other hand, excellence allows for failure, with a healthy outlook on growing from the experience and doing better next time round. The more you try, the more you are likely to succeed.

The battlefield is in the mind. Once you understand and grasp the fact that you have greatness within you,

you become unstoppable. No one can convince you otherwise, and grounded success becomes inevitable.

4)   PERCEPTION IS REALITY

How you look at things determines what you see and ultimately, what you get. There is an anecdote of the cathedral story that illustrates this perfectly: A man asks labourers what they are doing and one says, "I'm busting rocks and laying up bricks to earn a living", while the other says, "We are building a cathedral. Here is where the main auditorium will be, and the alter will be on this side", and goes on to explain all the features. From here we see that one is clearly shallow-sighted and will find the work laborious, while the other is long sighted and sees the pleasure in building something long-lasting for generations to come, for the pleasure and enjoyment of many. The latter man's perception affected his work ethic and attitude towards life because he focused on the outcome. He was goal oriented, enabling him to overcome any obstacles or challenges along the way knowing that the results are worth every effort and would serve a greater good. Attitude is everything.

Here are some ideas, adapted from Stephen Covey's book '7 Habits Of Highly Effective People', to demonstrate how a shift in perception from a negative to a positive paradigm can help bring about your desired success results:

1. **The Self -awareness Continuum:** the shift is from ineffective or irresponsible to proactive, taking responsibility and choosing response to condition or conditioning.

2. **The Imagination Continuum**: From victim or wandering to hope, purpose and pursuing passions.

3. **The Will power or Volition Continuum:** From coasting or floating to leverage and influence.

4. **The Abundance Mentality Continuum·** From limited pie or resources to profit, power, recognition for all, intrinsic self-worth, benevolent desire and mutual benefit.

5. **The Consideration or Courage Continuum:** From fight-or-flight instinct and wanting to be heard first - to two way communication, seeking first to understand, then to be understood, listening, restraint, reverence and empathy.

6. **The Creativity, Team-work or Synergistic Relationships Continuum:** From defensive - to compromise - to synergistic and creative alternatives to transformation.

7. **The Self-renewal, Self–improvement or Sharpening Continuum:** From entropy where everything breaks down to innovation, refinement and continuous improvement.

This Paradigm Shifted thinking produces energy-giving thoughts that move you away from negative energy-sapping thoughts, enabling the shift from scarcity to abundance.

Consciously create a healthy perception on purpose in order to create the reality that you want to experience in your life. For example, don't be stuck on a job seekers mindset. Think away from the herd. Divergent thinking makes you more creative and conspicuous, and this becomes a necessary component for grounded success. Brian Tracy says, "Your ability to think is the single most valuable asset and resource in this information age. Earning ability is the ability to apply knowledge and skill at the right time to get results that others are willing to pay for. Knowledge is the raw material for production and value in this age".

In his book, 'The Mis-education of The Masses', Wayne Malcolm beautifully illustrates how the education system has taught us to be dependent job seekers.

However, in this new economy it is important to realise that the era of job security has vanished. Our aim is to increase skills to the point where people are willing to pay the price that you set in exchange for your expertise and value.

Also, Robert Kiyosaki asserts that "the problem with a job is that relying on others to give you a living is the biggest risk of all". If you are employed, begin to see your employer as your client, the one you want to serve. That shift in thinking removes the burden of work and creates space for you to embrace and enjoy your vocation.

SUMMARY

You can see that what happens in your day is directly related to the expectation you put into it. Expect the best! The difference between not enough and more than enough is your attitude. So be the president of your fan club, expect the best in order to experience the best.

'Success or failure depends more upon attitude than upon capacity,' according to William James. Life is like coffee; savour the coffee, not the cup or container it comes in - jobs, careers, or businesses. Don't miss enjoying the coffee at the expense of trying to get the best cup. Here is a beautiful metaphor, to illustrate how you can go through difficult circumstances, but your reaction to it determines your resultant success in that area of your life:

We will take a look at three very different ingredients that display interesting characteristics before and after you subject them to boiling water: the egg, the carrot, and the coffee bean. The egg goes in fragile, with a thin outer shell protecting its liquid interior, but after boiling water, it becomes hardened on the inside. The carrot goes in strong, hard and unrelenting; however, afterwards, it is soft, soggy and becomes weak. The coffee bean however, infuses and penetrates the boiling water, causing it to change in appearance, taste and aroma. The ground coffee bean is unique as it totally changes the water rather than being affected by the water. Each of these objects faces the same adversity - boiling water, but each reacts differently.

Now ask yourself: Am I the carrot that seems strong, but with pain and adversity wilt and lose my strength? Am I the egg that starts with a soft heart, then after trials, become bitter, and resentful? Does my shell look the same, whilst being hardened on the inside? Or am I like the coffee bean that actually changes the hot water, the very circumstance that brings the pain? When the water gets hot, it releases the fragrance, flavour and colour of it.

So when things are at their worst, you get better and change the thinking around you. How do you handle adversity? Are you changed by your surroundings, or do you bring a new texture, flavour, aroma or colour to your environment? You decide.

REFLECTION POINTS:

I now invite you to go back into your childhood. Find out where it is that you got stuck in self-esteem and self-expression. Did they laugh at you because you gave the wrong answers in class? Or was it because you spoke with an accent, or you looked different from the rest of the other kids? Whatever it is, face that fear, denounce it as no longer a part of you or your destiny, and embrace the message that you carry within your voice. Let go of your past, in order to make room for new, positive, productive experiences that will enable you to enjoy Grounded Success.

Take an 'Attitude inventory' to see what's going on in your thoughts. Write down what you discover, and next to it, write down affirmations of the change you want to see in yourself. So for example if you discover that you are very critical and judgmental with people, write down the affirmation that: Wholesomeness emanates from my mouth; I accept others as they are, and I allow them to express their true authentic self.

'Imagination
gives you the
picture, Vision
gives you the
impulse to make
the picture
your own.'

SUCCESS
GRAVITY

CHAPTER 4

Vision

There is an African proverb that says, 'A seated old man will always see further than a standing boy'. Due to the depth of wisdom locked up in his grey hair, he has clarity of insight to move beyond just the physical sight to the inner sight of vision. Look beyond what you see.

I)   PUT ON YOUR SENSES! SIGHT VS VISION

What do I mean by vision? It's the Inner Senses of Hindsight, Insight and Foresight. It's good to acknowledge where you have been and understand where you are in order to know where you want to go. Hindsight enables you to understand the comfort zone from which you broke out of so you are not tempted to return. It becomes an uncomfortable place where everything in you will fight not to go back there again. A quote I love, by Mike Murdock, says 'your ignorance will recreate your crisis'. If you don't know that you don't know, chances are that subconsciously you will find yourself engaging in activities that take you right back to where you don't want to be. Hindsight will help you break free from that cycle.

Take a lottery winner, for instance. Let's assume that they are just an ordinary Joe Bloggs with no financial background or knowledge and they happened to buy the winning ticket. Statistics show that 94% of lottery winners file for bankruptcy within 24 months of the 'big win'. A psychological study reveals that subconsciously they begin to spend unnecessarily, and situations 'come up' which need a lot of money 'all of a sudden'. Eventually, their lifestyle reduces them back to the ordinary Joe Bloggs they were originally before the big win. Some end up even worse than when they were ordinary. What happens? Ignorance on the subject of money management will make them recreate their crisis.

Ignorance comes about where there is a lack of vision. Once someone has a vision in place, they do all they can to research and find the necessary resources to help them gravitate towards that vision to make it a reality. My favourite book says 'where there is no vision the people perish', meaning they cast off the discipline required in order for them to materialise that vision and hence perish or miss out on opportunities for success in that area. Ignorance is not bliss: it is blindness. It is darkness and it is tormenting; ignorance will cost you your happiness and stability.

If we look at our lottery example we find that the set of skills used to acquire money are different from the set of skills needed to manage that money, grow that money, invest that money, wisely distribute and spend that money. If acquiring it was all there was to it, we would all be rich millionaires. It's the amount of money you keep that matters, not the amount you get, and for that, you need skills. If you have played Monopoly before or Rich Dad's cash flow game by Robert Kiyosaki, you will know already that a low income earner, for instance a cleaner, can keep more money and hence come out of the rat race faster than a higher income earner such as a manager. What is the difference? Vision.

Insight gives a good picture of where you are now. Your vision will become clear only when you can look into your own heart. "He who looks outside dreams, he who looks inside awakens," Carl Jung observed. If you look with sight, you see things as they are, but if you look with insight you begin to see things as they could be. What is essential is normally invisible to the eye, so put on your internal specs of insight. Helen Keller, the famous blind poet, puts it this way: "It is a terrible thing to see and have no vision". Only he who can see the invisible can do the impossible.

An assessment of where you are now enables you to form a realistic picture of your present as well as provide you with the information you will require to know what resources you need to gather. Insight therefore asks, "Am I physically capable of walking towards this vision, or do I need the help of a vehicle to take me there?" If so what kind of vehicle? This could be a coach/mentor who has been where you want to go, or it could be a peer who says "let's take this journey together and see if we can get to this vision". The word insight is made up of two words - in and sight, meaning what is within immediate sight and where I am now, or what can I see in my present reality as it stands. The information then enables you to perceive what is possible. This process of grasping potential reality then leads to foresight.

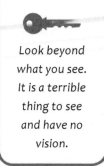

Look beyond what you see. It is a terrible thing to see and have no vision.

Foresight is about casting your inner eyes as far as you desire. It is about enlarging your capacity and horizons, looking at the possibility of an even bigger picture than you currently perceive. Napoleon Hill said, "Cherish your visions and your dreams as they are the children of your soul, the blueprints of your ultimate achievements".

As you go about your days, life seems to sing louder about your vision. Helpers of destiny begin to walk your way and as you walk towards your vision, it becomes larger and more tangible. Doors start opening of their own accord. The breakthrough is in taking steps towards it, and this comes with clarity of vision. For instance, when you stand at a distance from automatic sliding doors, they will not open until you are within a certain radius. However, once you step closer to where the sensors are, the doors open of their own accord. You don't need to stare at the doors, shout at the doors or use some special equipment or force - they just open as a result of complying with the 'scientific laws' by which they function. If these laws are violated they do not work. In the same way, taking bold steps towards your vision will enable you to walk through the doors with limitless possibilities.

2)   AVATAR: CHOOSE YOUR REALITY

The famous fictional hit epic movie 'Avatar', directed by James Cameron in 2009, has some enlightening parallels with real life. It is an action adventure journey of self-discovery in which the main character has a choice between fulfilling his assignment on earth to destroy the alien race called the 'Navi' (and remain bound in a wheelchair), or pursue his new found love in the second life for one of the Navi princesses, thus living a life of freedom and full expression where he has the power to do as he will (bearing in mind he is no longer wheel-chair bound). Drawing from this attention-grabbing phenomenon, I would like to submit to you that you can actually create and live your own Avatar as you perceive it.

What you perceive in your mind is what you will see a physical manifestation of.

So the question is, what do you see? Then what do you want to see? Don't play small with your answer, allow yourself to dream beyond your wildest imagination. Remember, you don't serve anyone by playing small. Some people think it is humility to play small. I say it is selfish. When you play big, see big, and strive to become big, you become a better person and are able to positively influence a whole lot more people in their lives. In other words, you can make a bigger impact, a bigger difference and contribution to other people's lives by becoming all you can possibly become. You begin to tap into your divine purpose because this is ultimately the big picture. You should see it as shameful if you were to die before you made your mark in this world; so refuse to die until you have done so.

When I was 10 years old I remember the summer holiday when my parents invited my cousins over to spend the holidays with us. The day was bright and sunny, and we were engaging in all the outdoor activities that you would expect from a group of 10 year olds. Meanwhile my dad had drained out the water from the pool in order to clean it out and put fresh water in for us to swim later. Whilst the water was still drained out, our little inquisitive minds told us to go and play in the empty pool and to 'not get caught' doing so. Our aim was to see who could do the best and latest dance moves. This of course came with the silently recognised title of being the 'coolest one' in the group! So after a few of us went round, it was my turn and I was determined with all my might to get the title. So there I was in an empty slippery pool, doing a dance called the 'running man'; you might have heard of it. Right in the thrill of showcasing my talent and with the biggest smile on my face, we all suddenly heard a loud bang! It was me; I had fallen flat on my face and broke my front tooth in half! It just had to be the front one! That smile soon turned into a panic as I knew I would get into trouble for ring leading an activity in which I knew we were not supposed to engage in the first place. I did not have time to cry and fortunately enough I was in no pain, although I could clearly see the piece of broken tooth in front of me. So we took our scared little wide eyed selves to my parents and told them what had happened. Good thing none of us got told off. Instead my mum immediately rushed me to our family dentist, Dr Zimmerman. From there the myriad dental visits began. My little 10 year old self fell in love with my dentist and his nurse who treated me like a princess every time I went for my appointments and healed my tooth painlessly, helping me restore that big signature smile once again. I can vividly remember this; it is fresh in my mind as though it just happened yesterday. Soon I began to get excited at just the smell of the dental materials; I would get exhilarated and come alive as soon as I approached the clinic.

Where misfortune would've had me physically marred and psychologically bruised, destiny spoke and gave way to the birthing of a new dream and passion in dentistry

I began to dream of becoming a dental professional when I grew up so that I could also make other people feel good about their teeth when they came to me. I began to envision myself in a white lab coat, drilling away, filling and polishing their teeth, taking x-rays and welcoming patients into MY surgery. Oh! That would keep me excited for hours.

So, where misfortune would've had me physically marred and psychologically bruised, destiny spoke and gave way to the birthing of a new dream and passion in dentistry. Today, many years on, I'm proud to be a qualified dental hygienist and therapist and I've worked in high end practices in London in which I've had the opportunity to treat celebrities from all over the world. Needless to say that I like to treat everyone like a celebrity. In retrospect, I remained true to my little 10 year-old vision of giving other people the same opportunity to have a good experience in dentistry as I had. This has helped me become a very popular and much sought after hygienist along with a loyalty following.

Beyond the reality of manifesting my Avatar, I later managed to set up my own dental practice in 2008 from scratch with a partner. We later moved on from there, however. I say all this to make the point that vision got me to where I am today. In high school, all the A-level subjects I took had to be in line with the vision I set as a 10 year old. The choice of moving to the UK and which universities to enrol in, all lined up with the vision. All the pre-qualification exposure and professional activities I engaged in had to line up with this vision which became more and more tangible the more I walked towards it. I grew into my Avatar. I came to a point where there was now no difference between the ideal picture I dreamt of and my reality. Now I have even bigger visions in both life and business, and I know the formula that works to achieve these. There is limitless power in having a strong vision, therefore, have a vision so strong that it pulls you towards it. Again I will ask you, what do you see?

3) VISUALISATION: A MODERN ART PHENOMENON

Clarity of vision becomes of utmost importance. When the rain and clouds disappear and sunshine comes through, it becomes clearer and brighter. It is easier to see. Clarity can also be achieved through writing down in words what you see or getting pictures that represent what you see. The latter describes the force and power behind visualisation. A lot has been written on this subject and basically visualisation is about constantly putting a picture of what you want to achieve before you. You could put up a vision board somewhere in your house or office where you're constantly reminded of what you want to see happen in your life or business. This vision board could have magazine pictures, photos or quotes of your vision. You could make your vision a screensaver on your computer or mobile device to engrave the picture into your subconscious mind, as it is constantly exposed to your conscious mind. Once a vision is clear it sets your subconscious search engine to work and things then seem to line up in your life to aid towards your vision.

As they say, when the student is ready the teacher shows up. The readiness of the student comes in the clarity of the vision to be materialised. Because your subconscious mind does not sleep, you begin to notice that your physical dreams may begin to line up or at least give you clues about your vision.

Brian Tracy asserts that there are four practical parts to the concept of visualisation. These are learnable and they ensure that you utilise this incredible power to your best advantage all the days of your life. I will share these here with you.

The first is *frequency* - **How often**. This entails the number of times that you visualise yourself performing excellently in a particular circumstance or event to achieve a particular goal. The more frequently you repeat a clear mental picture of your very best performance or result, the more rapidly it will become as part of your reality.

The second element is the *duration* - **How Long.** This relates to the length of time that you can hold the mental image in your mind each time you replay it. When you deeply relax, you can often hold a mental picture of yourself performing at your best for several seconds, and even several minutes. The longer you can hold your mental picture, the more deeply it will be engraved into your subconscious mind and the more rapidly it will express itself in your subsequent performance.

The third aspect is *vividness* - **How clear.** There is a direct correlation between mental clarity of your desired goal and the rapidness of its manifestation. The vividness of your desire directly determines how quickly it materialises in the world around you. An interesting phenomenon is that at the start of goal setting, your visual image may be vague, but in repetition, review and writing down, clarity is imbibed. Eventually, it becomes crystal clear to the extent that the goal will suddenly appear in your world exactly as you imagined it.

> *Once a vision is clear it sets your subconscious search engine to work and things then seem to line up in your life to aid towards your vision.*

The last element of visualisation is *intensity*- the **amount of emotion** that you **attach** to your **visual image.** In reality, this is the most important and powerful part of the visualisation process. Sometimes, if your emotion is intense enough and your visual image is clear enough, you will immediately achieve it. It is important to note that visualisation brings you whatever you vividly and intensely imagine, whether good or bad.

4)   IMAGINATION IS THE LIMITATION

'Imagination gives you the picture; vision gives you the impulse to make the picture your own', according to Robert Collier. This is where it gets interesting because the possibilities are endless. The vision is up to you and no one else can describe it better than you see it. It becomes a boundless, limitless place where only you can limit the vision. That's why it is said that you can take away everything from a man but you can never take away his dream or vision. This is where creativity is birthed, passion is ignited, inertia is overcome and you become an unstoppable force. Once a vision is put in place it is easier to move through obstacles because an earmarked destiny will always be within reach.

You start to see something others don't see, and get to know something others couldn't know, and therefore can capitalise on it before others see, know, or do it. Consequently, you develop the ability to do something others can't do either through knowledge, skill, or experience.

In business, there is a sociological model called the 'Adoption or Bell curve' developed by Rogers in 1962. This describes the adoption or acceptance of a new product or innovation according to the demographic and psychological characteristics of a defined group. It consists of five groups of people, namely Innovators, which make up 2.5% of the population; Early Adopters, 13.5%; Early Majority, 34%; Late majority,

34%, and finally the Laggards, making up 16% of the population.

Innovators and early adopters win, as they quickly capture the vision of a new product and innovation, due to their increased imagination. They see it with insight and seize it quicker. The quicker you can conceive a purposeful vision, the more likely you are to take advantage of it and succeed. As a visionary, you are then rewarded for strategy, rather than sweat.

SUMMARY

Do all you can, from where you are, with what you have. The vision sometimes becomes clearer, and is revealed as you go along and take the next step. Do not be afraid. This is why you need a new mind and new attitude first so that you can see it first before you seize it. A building is completed on paper first before it is finished physically. St. Augustine said, 'Faith is to believe what you do not see: The reward for faith is to see what you believe'. Visualisation then works as you walk towards what you see.

Your vision must encompass those that come after you. Have a vision so big and so far outreaching, that it cannot be completed in one generation alone. Offer your shoulders for future generations, having ensured that they have a solid foundation to stand and build upon. Isaac Newton himself said 'If I had seen farther, it is by standing on the shoulders of great giants'.

Where there is a vision, there is provision. Once you step out and head in the direction of your vision, you naturally begin to attract the resources necessary to carry out that vision, making Grounded Success inevitable.

REFLECTION POINTS:

Do some soul searching and introspection. Again I ask you, what do you see? What do you want to see? Allow your mind to go wild beyond imagination, for that is where the impossible will grow legs to become possible. Winston Churchill said 'there is nothing wrong with building castles in the air; so long as you build a foundation under them'.

ACTION POINTS:

Feed your mind continually with clear, exciting, emotional pictures. Set up a vision wall or vision board in your house where you can constantly see it. You can then cut out pictures, magazine images or use computer programmes with vision map software applications to help you create visual reminders of your vision. Use what most energises you.

'Truth crushed
to the earth,
will rise again...
undaunted.'

SUCCESS
GRAVITY

CHAPTER 5

Integrity

Integrity is the one value that is slowly eroding in today's society, and often overlooked, yet it is an integral part of life and business success. It is therefore necessary for me to put in all the synonyms associated with it in order to wedge in the gravitas of the concept.

Integrity embraces the principles of truth, character and honesty. It involves but is not limited to: openness, quality; quality assurance; beliefs; values; backbone; best practice; substance; brand honesty; ethics; code of conduct; good customer service; loyalty; virtues; distinction; originality; unique selling points; authenticity; away from herd mentality; genuineness; 360° leadership; no double standards; excellence; right motives; non-perfectionism but excellence; not self-centred but others-centred; non-compromising on quality; delivering your best value and content to your customers; compliance; current regulation, and adherence to legal, moral and ethical principles.

In business, integrity ensures that your value and content to customers and contractors, also measure up to other offerings in the marketplace. To stay relevant and provide best service with good quality standards that will benefit the customers. It speaks of caring about your customers, non-complacency, and commitment to continuous improvement. The Japanese introduced a strategic framework with a concept of continuous improvement called the 'Kaizen Philosophy'. Kaizen Principles can be adapted as a lifestyle, ensuring commitment to quality and lifelong learning that affects every area of your life. This will help to push you to become better in order to contribute better.

I)   LIFEBLOOD OF THE BODY

Everything that you do should reflect the integrity of who you are. We develop a depth in our purpose based on how we act in the smallest of small areas of our lives, in how we see, speak to and treat others.

In Thomas J. Stanley's eye-opening book "The Millionaire Mind", he shares a psychological look inside the mind, habits, and behaviours that led American millionaires to wealth accumulation and sustainability. Of all the traits, the one that most millionaires share is Integrity. In fact, they didn't just coincidentally share the same trait; they credit their integrity with significantly contributing to each of their successes. When you take a closer look at the reasons why integrity is key to achieving your goals, it goes much deeper than "good things happen to good people." After all, who would you want to do business with? Someone who is forthright, completely honest, and maintains an unwavering set of genuine principles? Or someone who will cut corners, tell you what you want to hear, lie to make the quick sale, then jump to their next customer? There are hundreds or thousands of people who design their business around making money at any cost. Many of them are out of business today. When you hold firm to principles and refuse to compromise them no matter what the brief payoff might be, you'll almost always win in the long term. Hold steadfast to your integrity when dealing with customers, employees, friends, and family. Soon you'll realise that people will go out of their way for your help, for your business ... for you.

Calamity is the test of integrity. Remember the story about the egg, coffee, and carrot? Well, the calamity of hot water brought out the true integrity of what was inside each of those elements, as the soft egg hardened, the coffee infused and the hard carrot softened. In the same manner, when you squeeze an orange, you should get orange juice as expected, and not lemon juice. Likewise, what you are on the outside should be congruent with what you are on the inside. That is true integrity.

Lead by example and be the change you want to see. We are what we repeatedly do and excellence is not an act but a habit. Set standards of excellence and accountability, doing things for the right reasons and motives. Even though sometimes I don't get the credit or recognition for the value I contribute in people's lives, I carry on because my motive is to serve and to see that positive difference in their lives. Be driven by empathy, compassion and altruism. See your work the way most others would view volunteering. So even if they didn't pay you for this difference you made, your quality and standards of service would still not be affected. You are your brand. Be truthful and faithful to the values you profess to live by in your mission statement. Honour your word and your promise to your customers. For instance, if you say you will contact them, do so at your earliest convenience. In business, always have a team ready, or virtual assistants to respond to enquiries, e-mails and even phone calls that same day. Stand by your guarantee. Be consistent - your actions must be consistent with the brand and promise.

When you hold firm to principles, and refuse to compromise them no matter what the brief payoff might be, you'll almost always win in the long term.

When I started to write this book I had to do a lot of soul-searching. I had to stay connected with the true purpose behind why I wanted to do all this and know that this would be my anchor and motivator to keep me focused to complete the project. The main purpose is to be able to give something back in other people's lives that is of value and has the capacity to positively impact their life for the good, and to shorten someone else's learning curve. I remember holding a conversation with my coach regarding this and a couple of things surfaced. Firstly, the desire to create something that is of value to others that would outlive me, and secondly, I had made a covenant with myself that I would not let my (10 year old) 'self' down. What I had promised that little girl back then, I would be faithful to fulfil: to maintain the integrity to myself in working on a dream and seeing it through until completion at all costs.

Maintaining integrity to myself is a value that I hold dear to my heart and I would encourage you to do the same. Jim Rohn said the only thing worse than lying to others is lying to yourself. When you can't trust yourself, how can you expect others to trust you if you can't keep your own promise to yourself? There is no hope for people to take you at your word. Gone are the days when someone was bound by their word alone. When one gave one's word, it was as good as done! Not so these days as we are forced to succumb to the notion 'seeing is believing'. We need to return to that place of integrity, truthfulness and backbone in our words and deeds. We also find that people tend to do good deeds with the wrong motives. Again this is not working in integrity as it is only a matter of time - or under sufficient pressure - before those wrong motives are exposed. We need to become people of our word, people of substance once again.

There is no higher value in society than integrity. R. Buckminster Fuller postulates that 'Integrity is the essence of everything successful'. I would go on to say it is the backbone that gives success its shape; it is the glue that holds other pieces together. It is the gravitational pull that keeps success firmly in place; the Lifeblood that keeps the body alive. 'If you have integrity, nothing else matters. If you don't have integrity, nothing else matters,' Alan Simpson observed.

2)   LAST MAN STANDING

Martin Luther King Junior said, 'Truth crushed to the earth, will rise again... undaunted'. Integrity is also about who you are and what you stand for. It's about your brand - Brand You. The message must be consistent. It is good to live your life in such a way that if wrong things are said about you, no one believes them because they know that whatever is said is out of character for you. Your reputation must go before you. Even if bad things are made up about you, it's only a matter of time before the truth surfaces. Integrity is also about under promising and over delivering, not vice versa. Let someone be impressed with the result of your promise as they had not expected it to be so good rather than disappointed that you've failed to meet their expectations after selling yourself so well.

At high school our motto was 'Veritas', meaning Truth in Italian. We were taught to be young people of truth and this was engrafted in us from the very beginning, as school principles to be adhered to. Why Veritas?

Well, this comes from the word verity, meaning not counterfeit or copied. They encouraged authenticity and originality in all our dealings. We had to walk in truth, be it in academics, sports or boarding school life in general. Truth prevailed. They were cultivating leaders of integrity and nurturing the virtue of truth in us. All this helped to create a backbone of integrity in our school culture and we were among the top schools with a high reputation and high pass rate. There were virtually no teenage pregnancies reported during my time at the school, and neither was there illicit drug use, violence nor police involvement concerning any of the students. We became a people of integrity and today, the motto of veritas has kept me in situations that I have had a choice to compromise. The option to pay the price of staying truthful is always more appealing even if it means I lose out on an opportunity.

Its about -
Brand You.
..It is good to live your life in such a way that if wrong things are said about you, no one believes them because they know that whatever is said is out of character for you

Integrity and openness help keep relationships genuine and healthy, be it in family life, friendships, or with co-workers and business associates. They say truth hurts but I say lies hurt even more as they destroy good relationships. Strive to be your authentic self, staying true to who you are and not being a counterfeit either. Our conduct speaks for us more eloquently than words ever could. Stand up for what is right, even if it makes you unpopular. There is an old hymn that has such powerful lines on integrity that go like this: 'Keep me true, Lord Jesus keep me true. There is a race I must run, there are victories to be won, give me power every hour to be true'.

We were taught to be young people of truth and this was engrafted in us from the very beginning, as school principles to be adhered to. We became a people of integrity and today, the motto of veritas has kept me in situations that I have had a choice to compromise.

This story's been told in many ways from an unknown source, so here is my version of it in relation to our discussion on integrity: I will call it 'Last man standing'. A successful businessman who was about to retire knew it was time to choose his successor to continue with the business. Instead of the obvious choice of either one of his sons or directors, he gathered all of his young company executives together. He told them his intentions, and gave each one a seed, with the following instructions: 'I want you to plant the seed, water it, and I want you to come back here, one year from today, with what you have grown from the seed I have given you. I will then judge the plants that you bring, and the one I choose will be the next Chief Executive Officer (CEO). So they all received the seed, and one man in particular, went home in excitement and told his wife, who helped him get a pot and soil in which to plant it. He watered it everyday and watched to see if it had grown and after 3 weeks, there was nothing. He heard the other executives talk about how their plants were budding and blossoming, but still, nothing was happening to his seed. Six months went by, and he diligently watered and fertilised the soil; still nothing.

However, he did not tell his colleagues as he did not want them to laugh at him.

When the year had passed and the day came for them to present their plants, the young executive was ashamed to take an empty pot. His wife, however, encouraged him to just be honest and not be embarrassed with what had happened. He took his empty pot to the boardroom, and was amazed at the beautiful variety of plants grown by the other executives. The CEO then arrived, greeted the executives and surveyed the room to see what each one had produced.

The young executive with the empty pot hid himself in the back with shame, entertaining the thought that everyone would think he was a failure and he might just get fired that day. To his amazement, the CEO sat everyone down and called him to the front and said, 'Behold, your new CEO'. The young executive could not believe it, and the rest wondered how this could be, since he couldn't even produce a simple plant within a year! Then the businessman explained, ' A year ago today, I gave each of you a seed, and commissioned you to plant it, water it, and bring it back to me. However, each of the seeds I gave you was boiled, so there was no way they could have grown. All of you except one substituted my seed when you found that it would not grow. He was the only one with courage and honesty enough to bring me a pot with my seed in it; therefore he will be the new CEO'. What a neat story of integrity!

3)   APPARENTLY TRANSPARENT

In these days of high technology and social media, it has become highly crucial to walk in integrity in life and business - to be transparent. Your online reputation is equally as important as your offline reputation. Once people find out inconsistencies about you, they withdraw business and connection with you at the click of a button.

What is a relationship after all, without trust and transparency? Integrity helps people realise when it is time to go separate ways in a peaceful manner. It is a sign of great maturity when you realise that your journey with someone is done and decide to end it honourably, without causing hurt. There is no time wasting for anyone and the release enables both parties to move on with their lives, fostering healthy relationships that serve them for the next level of their journey. From the previous example I gave in the relationships chapter, integrity, then, is about recognising who is the leaf, branch or root in your life, and letting go of the leaves and branches in a dignified manner. Integrity is about allowing yourself not to be a 'spare wheel' in someone's life and at the same time ensuring that they don't become burdensome to you or strain your energy, occupying a space that is meant to be taken up by a helper of destiny. As Shakespeare asserted, 'To thine own self be true'.

Practice excellence behind closed doors so that when it is demanded of you without warning, it shows up because that is what is etched on the inside of you anyway. This is what is referred to as Non-situational Integrity. Become a person of your word. Allow yourself to say no to tasks that you are unable to carry out, to be able to say no to people and not feel bad about it rather than say yes and make excuses later. It is better to say no then make an attempt at it later, than to say yes when you clearly know that you cannot execute the task. Walking in integrity ensures that you live a peaceful life as you are not constantly looking over your shoulder, running away from your own shadow or trying to cover up your tracks every time.

When your life is transparent you become apparent and begin to attract the right people in your life who will ensure you get to your destiny. In this microwave society that we live in, it is easy for one to ignore the virtue of integrity, creating cheap versions of products and services that are half-baked and unsatisfactory. This virtue seems to have been overlooked and this has translated into the lack of originality and creativity. We are finding more and more 'me too' companies and copycats arising and this kills imagination and growth. People have become lazy to research and hence find it easier to just become a cheap copy of an expensive original.

Thousands of people in the United Kingdom were mis-sold Payment Protection Insurance (PPI) policies by big lenders and banks. PPI is designed to cover repayments for a year, in the event of an accident, sickness or unemployment. Many of the companies lied or implied that it was compulsory, or sometimes even added it without telling their prospective customers. For online applications for instance, this would come in the form of a pre ticked box of which the applicant would not be aware. They did not explain the fine print to their customers, and made it seem like signing up for PPI was the only way to get a loan.

Your online reputation is equally as important as your off-line reputation

Now, a few years later, they are being asked to pay back in hundreds of thousands of pounds, as the financial ombudsman ruled in favour of compensating customers. Their lack of integrity has come back to bite them. One might say the PPI scandal came at the wrong time for banks since they're already experiencing an integrity-sapping crisis. However, truth always wins and there is never a better time to reap the rewards of dishonesty. It's a case of 'pay now or pay later', but either way you still pay. The latter pay is usually much higher and costs your reputation, in addition to any incremental damages and interest accrued as a result of trying to make short cuts. As the saying goes, 'a short cut is often a wrong cut'. Integrity therefore has no need of rules or exceptions - integrity is integrity, and as Arlen Specter affirms, 'Subtlety may deceive you, integrity never will'.

4)   THREE MUSKETEERS - LEGAL, ETHICAL, MORAL.

Integrity in life and business is also about working and walking within the legal and ethical parameters. The law has to be observed at all costs in order to avoid repercussions. In my profession, for example, I'm only allowed to practice the type of dentistry that I have received training for. I have a legal duty to work within my remit and anything outside of that becomes subject to litigation. It is not worth facing the consequences. Secondly, I have an ethical duty of care to first do no harm and make treatment options available to my patients. This will result in them making informed decisions that are in their best interest. The integrity of my service lies in the wording of information given and the emphasis placed on treatment options available to empower the patients. All this should be done with the patient's benefits in mind. The transparency of my service is reflected in the success rate of treatment and provision of sustainable after-care. There is also a moral obligation to act in benevolence to our fellow human beings for the greater good. This also ties in with the motives behind all actions carried out. Having a heart to serve will ensure that the right products and services are provided to our customer base with high quality that will guarantee a continued relationship in business transactions.

We recently had a visit from the Care Quality Commission (CQC) that is responsible for auditing and inspecting health organisations to ensure that high quality of care is provided to all patients. I was really proud of the fact that we did not need to run around much as all documentation was in order, all policies

an ethical duty of care to first do no harm

and procedures were transparent and accessible, and even random staff or patients that were interviewed had nothing but good to say about us. It says a lot about how we operate on a day to day basis. Ensuring good quality care is not just about having to upgrade operations for the auditors; we genuinely practice good dentistry and if they are to come unannounced they will find the same systems and standards in place. What you do when no one is watching is a reflection of who you truly are. As Oprah Winfrey put it, 'Real Integrity is doing the right thing knowing that nobody's going to know whether you did it or not'. You should strive for your character at work to be consistent with who you are at home or any other environment. Denis Waitley made an interesting discovery that there is no difference between personal and professional skills. People get fired for being late and disorganised, being rude or lazy.

Another anecdote to illustrate the importance of a heart of integrity goes like this: An elderly carpenter was ready to retire. He told his employer-contractor of his plans to leave the house building business and live a more leisurely life with his wife, enjoying his extended family. He would miss the pay cheque, but he needed to retire. They could get by. The contractor was sorry to see his good worker go and asked if he could build just one more house as a personal favour. The carpenter said yes, but in time it was easy to see that his heart was not in his work. He resorted to shoddy workmanship and used inferior materials. It was an unfortunate way to end his career.

When the carpenter finished his work and the builder came to inspect the house, the contractor handed the front door key to the carpenter. "This is your house," he said, "my gift to you." What a shock! What a shame! If he had only known he was building his own house, he would have done it all so differently. Now he had to live in the home he had built none too well.

So it is with us. We build our lives in a distracted way, reacting rather than acting, willing to put up less than the best. At important points we do not give the job our best effort. Then with shock we look at the situation we have created and find that we are now living in the house we have built. If we had realised that, we would have done it differently.

SUMMARY

We need to bring back Integrity to our families, communities, political, religious and economic institutions, educational systems, workforces and nations at large, one individual at a time. This is how whole nations can be restored.

In summary, I share this analogy of money. Whether you spit on it, fold it up, crumple it, stamp on it, or put dirt on it, it does not lose its value. It maintains its integrity no matter what is done to it. In the same way, no matter what circumstances we face, we must strive to maintain integrity. As mentioned before, some people are in your life for a reason, season or lifetime. So being true to yourself and your relationships will help you identify when the reason for that connection has been fulfilled and the season has shifted. Once you discern purpose, you can then gracefully move on to new levels in your life. This also applies to moving on from a group, association, a job or organisation. You give yourself a better chance at grounded success when you are true to yourself.

REFLECTION POINTS:

Think of yourself as the carpenter from the anecdote shared earlier. Think about your house. Each day you hammer a nail, place a board, or erect a wall, build wisely. It is the only life you will ever build. Even if you live it for only one day more, that day deserves to be lived graciously and with dignity. The plaque on the wall says, "Life is a do-it-yourself project." Your life tomorrow will be the result of your attitudes and the choices you make today. Choose Integrity in order to enjoy Grounded Success. Think about the situations in your life and business, where you have had to walk in integrity. Practice 'non-situational' integrity.

ACTION POINTS:

Make a firm decision now, and put it in writing, that at all costs and to the best of your ability, you will live a life of integrity.

'Do you love
life? Then don't
squander your
time for this is
the stuff that life
is made of.'

SUCCESS
G R A V I T Y

CHAPTER 6

Time Management

We're living in a world where values and principles of life and business are constantly changing at a fast pace. In order to keep up or at least to survive comfortably, I believe it is important to pay attention to the invaluable resource of time. This is the only resource that we all have as human beings in equal access and measures. However, the use of it is up to us. We trade the intangible time for everything tangible we have in our lives, for instance work, cars and houses.

Time has different dispensations. It speaks of days, ages, or seasons; to everything is a season, a time for every purpose. It is also good to be aware that the timing of the project is equally as important as managing the time to do it. For instance, starting a building project in the rainy season is a guarantee for failure as the building materials remain moist and are not exposed to the right elements that bring about integrity of the structure. Understanding the concept of time, therefore, increases awareness of timing events appropriately - or what is called acting in the fullness of time. It's not enough to just know what to do; it is equally important to know when to do what you need to do.

I)   POWERFUL PERISHABLE RESOURCE

Time is a perishable resource that needs to be managed well. When you come to realise that life is not a

'Do you love life? Then don't squander your time for this is the stuff that life is made of' - Benjamin Franklin.

rehearsal for the real act, but the actual play itself in which you are the main character, time becomes of essence and begins to take on a brand new meaning. You clocked into time the day you were born, and since then, the clock is ticking with irreplaceable time, racing towards eternity. Anything else can be recycled, not time. This is to help bring an awareness of morality that will enable you to take stock of your life in order to allocate your time to what truly matters to you and adds to the fulfilment of your purpose.

You begin to see the direct correlation between happiness and time. What does this mean? A lot of people go to work for endless hours or engage in business in order to build the life of their dreams, which usually entails spending quality time with friends and family, doing the things they love. In essence, people go to work to buy time. Time then becomes an invaluable resource that requires management. How you choose to spend your day, week, month, year and lifetime is a reflection on how you respect time or the lack of it. Who you choose to spend your time with also measures and reflects the importance you place upon that individual. What you spend your time on indicates the value you place upon it, as it becomes a mirror to reflect your own character and attitude. There are so many misconceptions we hear about time. One of the common ones is: 'time is money'. But time is time and money is money. In fact the more important resource is time because you can spend money and make some more but once time is gone it is gone.

Anything else can be recycled, not time. This is to help bring an awareness of morality that will enable you to take stock of your life in order to allocate your time to what truly matters to you and adds to the fulfilment of your purpose.

Research on relationships shows that when children are asked what they like or don't like about their parents, they almost always go back to the amount of time spent with them, and the activities they do or don't do together. These include such things as being there to watch the game or play at school, playing soccer or dolly house together, dancing around or playing instruments together, or teaching them how to ride a bike.

Their responses rarely relate to the presents they were bought, the clothes they got or the food they ate. It's the intangible gift of time that translates to love and care for them; it translates to being there for them. In his book 'The Five Languages of Love', Gary Chapman highlights this interesting phenomenon of love languages spoken and understood by people differently. The list of love languages include: gifts, acts of service, words of affirmation, physical touch and quality time. Your job is to learn the language of love of your children, spouse, friends or associates and then speak that love language. Quality time is synonymous with love.

2) PROCRASTINATE PROCRASTINATION!

Lurking at every street corner is a thief, ready to steal at any given opportunity. It creeps in slowly, unannounced and is the kind that hardly draws attention to itself. I am referring to procrastination, the thief of time. It robs you of your time and ultimately steals your destiny. Procrastination is the disease that comes in undetected and spreads like a cancer. Your job is to check in with yourself and examine your habits and attitude towards your commitments. This ensures that you make an early diagnosis to cure this terrible disease of putting off things until tomorrow or another time. They say a goal without a deadline takes forever, and forever never happens. Knowing that procrastination is a habit means that it is something learned and can therefore be unlearned. How? By replacing the habit.

The best way to change a habit is not by stopping it, but by replacing it. A lot of research has gone into this, where scientists have studied smokers, for instance. They have proved time and again that it is the replacement of the habit that brings about victory as opposed to the many attempts at stopping it. We are all creatures of habit and the antithesis or medication for procrastination is massive action towards the desired goal.

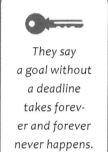

They say a goal without a deadline takes forever and forever never happens.

I can't tell you the number of ways in which I have procrastinated writing this book. Doing the necessary research and applying the required discipline to see it through was a challenging test. Again I knew I had to practice what I was preaching and apply the principles I was going to share with you. You will find that all the keys shared in this book are tried and proven by myself and others. I have had to face the challenges in life, and writing this book has qualified me to speak from a point of experiential knowledge. Now, you do not necessarily have to take massive action every day, but small baby steps towards a desired outcome are enough to keep the monster of procrastination at bay. Small steps, for example, could be writing a to do list or making a single phone call to an accountability partner who will ensure that you carry out your commitments to yourself.

Reading one page of a book chapter, filling in the application form, buying the newspaper with the job offer - all these are small steps. Also, when you constantly have a clear picture of the end in mind to remind you of your desired outcome, you become more motivated to take action when you realise that the goal is not going to achieve itself; it requires you to make it happen. Small action steps ensure that you are not overwhelmed to inertia, where you end up not doing anything at all. Larger projects can be broken down into smaller, manageable steps to stop you from feeling overwhelmed. Also, taking small breaks in between is important for energy renewal.

Procrastination, complacency, and indecision are the arch-enemies of speed. On the highway, speed kills, whereas in business, in finances, and in accomplishing your goals, speed wins every time. So if you decide you want to become more fit, don't wait until Monday. Create your plan now. Then, seconds after now, start working out. Then, immediately after your workout, plan your next one. If you respect time, time will respect you and give you back fruits of results.

3)   PROPER PRIOR PLANNING PREVENTS POOR PERFORMANCE

Proper prior planning and preparation prevents poor performance. Be prepared. If you fail to plan, you plan to fail. Writing things down prior to doing them helps to identify where there may be 'resource gaps' that need to be filled. Instead of running around looking for help on the day it is much easier to know beforehand what you need, what resources are necessary and how to access them. This also gives room to tweak what is not working and make adjustments that allow you to meet the target within the time frame you had set for yourself. In order to manage your time it is good to plan ahead of time. Planning when the time is due is probably going to overwhelm you, put you off and kick you into procrastination mode. So before anything is due, plan ahead of time for it. One of my teachers used to say "...'on-time'... is late!".

If you arrive for a meeting at 9 o'clock that is due to start at 9 o'clock, that is late. Why? You may need to meet and greet, get comfortable, get the necessary documentation or apparatus required for the meeting, fumble to find your phone and switch it off, and all the little things that need to be done prior to the meeting. You also need to de-stress and focus yourself to be fully present for the meeting. By the time all that is done it could be a good 10 to 20 minutes wasted. Instead, arrive early so that when it is time to start, the meeting starts. Time management helps with stress management. You are able to see the need to delegate tasks that others can do on your behalf, and by so doing, you can then dedicate more of your time to high productivity activities that others cannot do for you.

This leads me to my next point about productivity. It speaks of tangible results. Some people are known to be busy bodies, ever running around but with nothing to show for it at the end of the day, like a hamster in a wheel. You should not confuse aimless activity with productivity. One just expends energy and leaves you fruitless, while the other produces tangible, measurable results.

Planning ahead means planning your day, week, month, year, and the next five to 10 years. Successful companies that have been around a long time have 50 year plans. The night before the following day is a good time to reflect on the day, assess how you managed your time and then make a to-do list for the following day, so that when it arrives you are not wasting time starting from scratch. This saves time and increases the likelihood of success and completion of those tasks because already your mind becomes alert to resources that will ensure execution of the task. As we said in Chapter One on goal setting, your reticular activating system is activated and your subconscious search engine starts to work on your behalf as you sleep or dream.

This is about making back up plans, or forecasting what may go wrong and putting strategic plans in place to make sure it doesn't go wrong. It involves planning for an unexpected out come as a safeguard, or a means of risk management.

In his book, '21 Irrefutable Laws of Leadership', John. C. Maxwell outlines how to plan ahead using the acrostic PLAN AHEAD. These are profound insights on time management that I'm hoping you will find useful: P- Predetermine a course of action; L- Lay out your goals; A- Allow time for adjustments, because you will need to make them; N- Notify key personnel involved in your project; A- Allow time for acceptance, because change in plans ask for it; H- Head into action; E- Expect problems, because you may have them when you go for the action; A- Always point to the successes, because somebody will always point to your failures, and lastly, D - Daily review your progress.

This leads me to another crucial element of Contingency Planning. This is about making back-up plans, or forecasting what may go wrong and putting strategic plans in place to make sure it doesn't go wrong. It involves planning for an unexpected outcome as a safeguard, or a means of risk management. You will find that, for example, many operational businesses will have generators as a backup when there is a sudden power failure or power cut which could potentially cost the company a lot of money. This ensures that the business continues running as normal, without having to experience the loss or damage caused by the temporary lack of electricity. Although contingency planning is normally connected to larger scale disasters like floods, tornadoes and fires, what would happen if a main supplier of a company suddenly went bankrupt, or the entire sales force got sick from food poisoning at a work conference? It is therefore important to incorporate contingency planning as part of everyday operations in terms of business and have an awareness of this on a personal level.

4)   PRODUCTIVITY- THE PARETO PRINCIPLE

Don't confuse activity with productivity. Fumbling your thumbs or rocking in a chair is activity, but it doesn't get you anywhere. Therefore, concentrate on results, not on being busy. Saying this however, doing something towards your goal and getting it wrong is at least ten times more productive than doing nothing at all. You end up regretting the things you did NOT do in life, far more than the things you did.

Often when people have feelings of regret and unfulfilled lives, it's because they look back over a period of their life and realise how long they wasted time in fruitless activities or habits. This can even be down to internal traits like bitterness, unforgiveness and holding on to past hurts and grudges. Worse still is when they realise they could have done something to improve their lives, and they didn't. This all accrues to lost time that can never be found. Opportunities would have been missed as a result of embracing unproductive habits.

The 80/20 rule of productivity states that 80% of our activity or unfocussed effort accounts for 20% of the results achieved. The remaining 80% of results are achieved with only 20% of the effort. This broad pattern of a small proportion of activity generating non-scalar returns recurs so frequently as to be the norm in many areas of life. Take for example your wardrobe: you will find that 20% of the clothes in your wardrobe are worn 80% of the time, while you hardly wear the rest. On average, 80% of what we hear in a classroom setting results in 20% of knowledge retention. That is why it is important to keep yourself exposed to the subject in order to retain more.

Being aware of the 80/20 rule and applying it keeps you focused on those activities that will produce the biggest measures of results. You can therefore optimise your effort to ensure that you concentrate as much of your time and energy on high payoff tasks. This also ensures that you achieve the greatest possible benefit with the limited time available to you. Some people assume that multitasking is a great phenomenon for completing many projects at once. This is a myth because attention is divided and the power of focus is lost. Laser focus on one goal or project at a time is what ensures results. In as much as you may want to complete many projects at once, the likelihood is that you will have many uncompleted, half baked projects that just reflect how disorganised you are. For example, it would be odd for someone to

The 80/20 rule of productivity states that 80% of our activity or unfocussed effort, accounts for 20% of the results achieved. The remaining 80% of results are achieved with only 20% of the effort

dig a foundation then stop and dig another foundation and keep doing the same. They would just end up with a bunch of dug foundations and no actual completed building project. It is better to take your time and do what it takes to complete one task before moving onto the next. That way you get enough momentum to attempt the next task, while also gaining self-respect as well as that of others. Make time for Grounded Success.

The following story beautifully illustrates the importance of time management in relation to your allocation of time: A professor stood before her Philosophy class and had some items in front of her. When the class began, wordlessly, she picked up a very large and empty mayonnaise jar and proceeded to fill it with golf balls.

Laser focus on one goal or project at a time is what ensures results -you achieve the greatest possible benefit with the limited time available to you.

She then asked the students if the jar was full. They agreed that it was. So the professor picked up a box of pebbles and poured them into the jar. She shook the jar lightly. The pebbles, of course, rolled into the open areas between the golf balls. She then asked the students again if the jar was full. They agreed it was.

The professor then picked up a box of sand and poured it into the jar. Of course, the sand filled up everything else. She then asked once more if the jar was full. The students responded with a unanimous- yes. The professor then produced two cans of liquid chocolate from under the table and proceeded to pour the entire contents into the jar effectively filling the empty space between the sand. The students laughed. "Now," said the professor, as the laughter subsided, "I want you to recognise that this jar represents your life. The golf balls are the important things: your family, your spouse, your health, your children, your friends, your favourite passions; things that if everything else was lost and only they remained, your life would still be full.

"The pebbles are the other things that matter like your job, your house, your car. The sand is everything else, the small stuff. If you put the sand into the jar first, there is no room for the pebbles or the golf balls. The same goes for your life. If you spend all your time and energy on the small stuff, you will never have room for the things that are important to you. Pay attention to the things that are critical to your happiness. Take care of the golf balls first, the things that really matter. Set your priorities. The rest is just sand," she said.

One student raised her hand and inquired what the chocolate represented. The professor smiled. "I'm glad you asked. It just goes to show you that no matter how full your life may seem, there's always room for chocolate!"

SUMMARY

Wherever I go, I hear most people say the same thing, 'I would love to do it, but I just don't have enough time'. Even if they know it's important and could make a difference, they are totally overwhelmed by their current tasks, and the thought of working on one more thing is just too much for them.

So why is there such a lack of time? An online survey reveals some of the top seven reasons:

1. Someone else sets your agenda and fills your schedule with tasks.

2. You don't know what to say 'no' to and how to say 'no'.

3. Because we can do so many things these days, we do that in multitasking.

4. We want to keep an eye on everything because the world is complex and changing and we are constantly distracted.

5. Our physical workspaces encourage distractions.

6. We are more connected than ever and technology keeps the channels open.

7. Being generalists, we tackle new things over and over and never really get proficient.

REFLECTION POINTS:

What have you been procrastinating in your life? Maybe it is time to take baby action steps towards it.

These suggestions will help you take control of your time: Firstly, learn a task management method of getting things done by having a 'to do' list. Next, understand your priorities and work out how your work fits in to the big picture. If it doesn't fit in to either the big picture or your priorities then say 'no'. Also, get into a community of practice and learn how to work smarter from your peers and those already doing it. Rather than try and keep up with all the changes in your discipline, share the workload. Lastly and maybe most importantly, periodically close down all communication channels. Turn off the mobile, Skype, email and then find a cafe where you can work anonymously. You'll be amazed at how much work you'll get done.

ACTION POINTS:

As part of a daily productivity practice, write down answers to these questions:

1. What three high impact-producing activities will I get done today?
2. What three high income-producing activities will I get done today?
3. Whose help do I need and who needs my help today?

'The key to
realizing a dream
is to focus not
on success but on
significance- and
then even the small
steps and little
victories along your
path will take on
greater meaning.'

SUCCESS
GRAVITY

CHAPTER 7

Your Contribution

As discussed in goal setting, it is good to begin with the end in mind and make strategic steps to get there, soliciting help along the way from peers, mentors and other achievers or role models. The sequence of the 'Success Gravity' formula with Y (Your contribution) being at the end is no coincidence, as I believe the ultimate goal of success is to share it with others. This is the completed picture of Grounded Success. It's about making a difference to people's lives with that success, and making a contribution towards improving their quality of life also. Aside from this, success becomes a selfish gain. This is why there is so much resentment from those in your sphere of influence when you become successful. This is also why most successful people are soon forgotten with their success when they die. Due to having had no impact or significance in other people's lives, there is nothing left for others to celebrate or build upon. Charity may begin at home, but if it does not go further, it ceases to be charity and becomes mere clan loyalty.

'Your character is more important than your career, and nothing builds character more than generosity,' Jim Rohn observed. When you are able to look outside yourself, to help someone else, it makes of you a better you.

1)   SHOW ME YOUR BIRTH CERTIFICATE!

Ever asked yourself the question why was I born? What is my purpose, legacy or mission on this earth? Well, the answer is normally found in what frustrates you the most that you love to fix, what injustices you resonate with that eventually become a cause for you to fight and stand up against. In a nutshell, such issues represent the problem you were created to solve. A life with a cause is the cause of life, so aim to leave this world in a better state than you found it. We all have a mandate to contribute something positive to our world that in turn impacts the whole world.

He noted that first came the date of her birth and spoke of the following date with tears, but he said what mattered most of all was the dash between those years

While your birth certificate represents physical evidence of your existence, greater and more significant evidence yet is the impact that you make in the world around you through your positive contribution. Apart from this, your birth certificate just becomes a meaningless piece of paper. You show that you are alive by the deeds that you do and the difference that you make. Even when a baby is born, they all wait for that all-important cry that announces that they are alive. The baby is able to contribute positively to that environment, bringing joy to those around it by "yelling out" its existence. So if a baby can contribute, then surely you stand a chance at making a significant contribution to your world.

A famous poem called 'The Dash' by Linda Ellis will help shed light on how you can consciously begin to live your life on purpose, and add meaning to your birth certificate. Here it goes:

> I read of a man who stood to speak
> at the funeral of a friend.
> He referred to the dates on her
> tombstone, from beginning to the end.
> He noted that first came the date of her
> birth and spoke of the following date
> with tears.
> But he said what mattered most of all
> was the dash between those years.
> For that dash represented all the time
> that she spent on earth.
> And now only those who loved her
> know what that little line is worth.
> For it matters not how much we own,
> the cars, the house, the cash.
> What matters is how we live and love
> and how we spend our dash.
> So think about this long and hard, are
> there things you would like to change?

For you never know how much time
is left that can still be rearranged.
If we could just slow down enough to
consider what's true and real.
And always try to understand the
way other people feel.
And be less quick to anger and show
appreciation more.
And love the people in our lives
like we've never loved before.
If we treat each other with respect
and often wear a smile.
Remembering that this special dash
may only last a while.
So when your eulogy is being read,
with your life's actions to rehash.
Would you be proud of the things they
say about how you spent YOUR dash?

How very profound!

2) LEGACY - LIVE IT TO LEAVE IT

Think generationally; have a 200 year plan. There
is no success without succession. When you realise
that you are a part of something much bigger than
yourself, your whole outlook on life changes. Your
contribution is something that should outlast you.
Therefore, build a lasting legacy, something beyond
yourself.

Again, how would you like to be remembered when you leave this earth?

I currently serve as Vice President for our Toastmasters International Speaking Club, and during my term, I have come to realise a couple of things I would like to share with you. There is so much joy in volunteering time and service to keep the club running, without getting monetary remuneration. This becomes our contribution to the club beyond the club meetings. Secondly, when I see a totally nervous person with more butterflies in their tummy than in the field, begin to speak up, transform and blossom at the encouragement of the club, it is one of the most exhilarating experiences that remind us of why we do what we do. A speech can make such a huge impact on individuals, in terms of style, delivery, and content that it makes you unforgettable forever! It can become your legacy.

At the risk of sounding morbid, I would like you to imagine your date of death. They have all gathered around and your casket is right there in the middle of them. What will they say about you? Hero? Fallen Soldier? Good riddance? Gone too soon? What would they say in relation to how you live your life right now? Will it be just a few that mourn and feel the impact of the absence, or will it be the masses - the many lives that you have touched? Will they still talk about you long after you have gone? Now having truthfully reflected on this, what do you want them to say about you? What ever it is you want them to say, start making the necessary adjustments to live your life that way. In other words, live your legacy now so that later you can leave the legacy that you had lived on purpose. This is not about people pleasing either. You shape up in people's minds how you want to be remembered. This is how you live your life authentically on purpose. You work your way backwards from your date of death and trace those steps to your present day reality, crafting out the life that you desire to live.

George Bernard Shaw put it this way: 'Life is not about finding yourself but about creating yourself'. Therefore, create yourself! Create the life that you desire. If you can begin to see your purpose as something you grow into, you create a new appreciation for the life you design to live out, as opposed to look for. You don't get to it, as it is not a destination, but rather you grow into it. The challenge is not in acquiring that life, but the key is accessing it. You already have it within you. It is time to harness it.

It's up to you to take full responsibility and ownership of your life. It doesn't matter how ugly your past has been. Whether anyone did something to you in the past or you suffered negative experiences - such as being hurt, abused, impoverished, raped, rejected, addicted, or being misunderstood- it's not what happens to you but how you react to what happens to you that counts. They had your past, but you can take back your present and your future. Make a decision to own it. The word 'decide' comes from the root word that means to cut off. Therefore, cut off all the opinions they have of you, and say to yourself; 'this is my life, I only have one life and I want to make this one count'. Commit to that promise and you will find that life has a way of cooperating with you once you make that decision. Tony Robins says "It's in your moments of decision that destiny is shaped". Therefore decide your destiny. The notion of predestination annoys me. The statement that 'if it's meant to be it will be', is loathsome to me. It takes away all responsibility and you end up just living your life on a reactive level. That is the lowest form of animal instinct, the lowest form of intelligence. Life must be proactive, planning ahead the outcomes you wish to see. I subscribe to the notion 'if it's meant to be it's up to me!' Make it happen; take life on. Aspire to inspire before you expire; live your legacy on purpose so you can leave it when you depart.

3)   IMMORTALITY - YOUR BEST SHOT BEYOND THE GRAVE

There are many great orators whose words still speak today, even though they have long departed this earth. Words that will still speak to generations yet unborn. Their contribution has enriched our lives for the better for example, Martin Luther King Junior's 'I have a dream' Speech. Similarly, those who write books, or compose songs or poems, ensure their place in recorded history. That's about as good as it gets with immortality. This is how can you make yourself 'immortal', so to speak. There are great legends of our time that still speak beyond the grave. In our time, we've had: Steve Jobs, Whitney Houston, Jim Rohn, Zig Ziglar, and from times gone, we still hear the voices of: Elvis Presley, John F. Kennedy, Franklin D. Roosevelt, Albert Einstein and Isaac Newton to name a few - still speaking beyond the grave.

A book, like a song or speech, for example, makes you immortal in a sense, because long after you have departed, the words in the book will still speak to different generations especially if the message is age-less. A book goes to countries you may never be able to travel to, speaks to audiences you may never meet and now with the Internet, e- books have the potential to touch millions of lives in a very short space of time. We have many examples of video clips that have been uploaded with dance or song or speeches that have become viral within seconds. They are all ensuring their place in history. The world has become a stage and people are making visible, accessible, lasting impact as a result of this.

4)   SUCCESS TO SIGNIFICANCE

'The key to realising a dream is to focus not on success but on significance - and then even the small steps and little victories along your path will take on greater meaning'- Oprah Winfrey .

Success alone is not enough. That can be rather selfish. The limited pie or scarcity mentality is a myth. Robert Kiyosaki puts it this way: "When you create wealth, it is your responsibility to return it to society". Give your gift, serve others and you will be taken care of in abundant ways. Your contribution does not always have a monetary value. It could simply be deciding how you want to show up in the world and how you want to serve. In the pursuit of my significance goals I have decided to show up and position myself as a midwife. What do I mean? I have decided to be there as a mentor and coach for someone else needing a hand to materialise their dream. The concept of your contribution rests on the premise that in as much as someone else has contributed into your life for you to be where you are, you have a duty to reciprocate that and make a contribution to someone else's life. As you have freely received, freely give. This has got to be beyond your immediate call of duty and responsibility i.e. friends and family or people you can benefit from. It goes beyond your inner circle to the wider circle of the community, society, country, continent and world at large, having a sort of ripple effect.

Now this should not be overwhelming, as the world has now been shrunk through the Internet, media and digital communications. We are now able to significantly impact and reach out to the world online as well as offline. Now the little man can surely get ahead and make a difference! We have witnessed how people are now using social media strategies, for example, to get ahead in life and become famous from the backside of nowhere. Great lifestyle opportunities have been created for ordinary people to arise to fame and fortune in this new economy, where previously there were high barriers to entry. We find that individuals can now build a list of followers that buy into their message and buy their products as well, at no cost to low cost. At the same time, the big advertising companies are not trusted anymore. They have been proven to fall short with their services and promises. As individuals or small companies, it's easy for people to gain a clearer picture of who you are through social proof and feedback from others who have used your services. There are no longer any gate-keepers preventing you from making it big. The barriers to entry have been removed. There are therefore no excuses for anyone not to make an impact in their world.

The concept of your contribution rests on the premise that in as much as someone else has contributed into your life for you to be where you are, you have a duty to reciprocate that and make a contribution to someone else's life

I am committed to walking alongside individuals who feel they don't have a voice, to help them find their voice and let them know it's okay to speak up. These may be people who are shy to speak, or have low self esteem, stemming from abuse, rejection, ridicule, oppression, judgement, despair or shame. Whatever the case, they too have something to say. Now the word voice can also be seen as a metaphor to mean what you have to say through your life or what you have to give. The voice of Mother Teresa, who helped destitute people on the streets of

Calcutta, spoke of kindness; Martin Luther King Junior's voice spoke about dreams of human freedom and racial equality; Nelson Mandela's voice speaks of forgiveness. We all have a message in our voice and we all want our voices to be heard. I recently gave an award winning speech entitled 'Speak up! There is a message in your voice!' In it I touched on these elements and the results of that speech were that people were inspired to go back to their childhood to see what it is that stopped them from speaking up. This helped to break deep-rooted emotional and psychological hindrances for some, while others then came up to me to ask for my mentorship. It is one of the most humbling experiences when this happens, as it reminds me that I'm living my purpose which is to bring out the best in others - being that 'midwife' so to speak. I love to help people tap into themselves and bring out the dreams that they have locked up on the inside of them, to help unlock purpose-connected dreams, hopes and ambitions.

My voice speaks of encouragement, determination, inspiration and motivation. Here is my personal mission statement: "As I help individuals connect to their purpose, I aim to inspire, encourage, motivate and cultivate the best out of them, so that they can create their dream lifestyle". We should all have a personal mission statement that lines up with the vision and values we have in life. This helps you not to lose your way and quickly find it if you do. When storms of life hit, you have an unshakable foundation because your mission is there like a satellite navigator, to help you find your path once again.

Live a life of significance; therein lies true success. They say true success is not measured by the amount of possessions acquired, but by the number of obstacles overcome. When you keep grounded in your contribution, you realise that the source of true wealth is in giving. Giving starts the receiving process, it's a cycle. When you sow a seed and do the necessary work, receiving a harvest is inevitable. Michael Jackson, for instance, could have just danced by himself in his bedroom and kept all those remarkable moves to himself. However, no one would have known him at all and he wouldn't have made the impact in the world that he did. Some of his early lyrics spoke to the world mainly about creating peace and harmony. His dance moves have shaped the music industry's visual entertainment today. It took him endless hours to perfect a dancing skill, then showcase and share his moves with the world for entertainment and subsequently adaptation. He made his contribution to the world.

SUMMARY

1) Decide on a goal you want to achieve. No one can stop the power of a made up mind; 2) Work out what relationships and networks you will need to help you attain that goal, for instance, masterminds, alliances, circles to join, books to read, blogs or people to follow on the internet; 3) Maintain a positive mindset and attitude against all odds, staying determined while looking out for any blind spots, pitfalls or challenges

you may encounter in pursuit of your goal; 4) Have a clear image (visualisation) and vision of what the picture of success in achieving your goal looks like. Let it be a constant reminder and motivator for you; this becomes an anchor to help keep track and enable helpers of destiny to aid you towards the same clear goal; 5) Ensure that you work with integrity towards this goal, not compromising your character, beliefs or values in the process and being mindful not to purposefully infringe on the rights of others as well; 6) Manage your time wisely and strategically, taking daily steps towards your goal. Also, plan ahead to eliminate any stress and being overwhelmed, avoiding procrastination; 7) Bear in mind what kind of impact your goal will have on others and how it can improve not only your life, but quality of life for others as well. Finally, when your goal is achieved, celebrate and share your success in that goal with others, so that it's not just about you. Move from a success paradigm to a significance paradigm. Herein lies the fulfilment of life and business that we so often seek and desire.

When success is shared, it has more meaning just like sharing a cake or a meal. Most successful people in life start companies or organisations. In doing this they provide employment and education opportunities for other individuals who are then able to provide for their families. Winston Churchill put it well when he said, 'We make a living by what we get and we make a life by what we give'.

REFLECTION POINTS:

I challenge you to reflect upon this definition of purpose: 'Purpose is that thing within you, that pulls the best out of you, to unleash the best around you'. Read that again. What is it for you?

When you were born, you were the only one crying and everyone around you was smiling. Live your life in such a way that when you die, everyone around you is crying and you are the one who is smiling. Then you can say, 'Mission accomplished, baton passed, legacy well lived and left behind'.

ACTION POINTS:

List out your talents, passions and values and ask yourself how you can use them to serve others or make a bigger contribution. Sometimes we are good at what we do, but we still aren't using our gifts and talents. When we tap into those and use them, we feel a greater sense of satisfaction. Write down how those talents and gifts may be used as service to other people, where no monetary value is involved. Write out your personal mission statement, taking mine as an example of how you may want yours to read.

SUCCESS
GRAVITY

CONCLUSION

Outro

In order to write this book, I've had to have a vision, write down clearly defined goals with the correct plan of action, manage my time wisely, and maintain a positive attitude. I've had to overcome writer's block, fear and 'overwhelm', network with coaches, mentors, and mastermind alliances. I've liaised with friends, maintained the integrity and essence of the book, shared my authentic truths, and also had to remember that this is my contribution towards a lasting legacy that will linger long after I have departed this earth. I had to apply the exact same principles and the proof is in the pudding, as you are reading this very book! Success for me in this respect was two-fold: Firstly, the completion and manifestation of this book. Secondly, the amazing testimonials of how the book itself is bringing clarity to people who are not quite sure what vocational path to take in their lives to produce success on personal, professional and global levels. This I am trusting to be true for you as you have picked up the book and read it hopefully as a success guide, manual or reference point to lead you towards the path that will take you where You want to go.

To reiterate the principles shared in this book, I will use the metaphor of someone building a house. Goals are like the raw materials required to build the house. Without these, you and I both know that it will be a mere wish and frivolous activity that can never transpire into anything tangible. Relationships are the various professionals required to build this house: from architects to plumbers, builders to designers, surveyors to inspectors, electricians to decorators; all the disciplines involved. Attitude is like the windows and doors; these are portals of entry and exit, controlling what goes in and what comes out. Vision is the blueprint or architectural drawing. You cannot build without it because in the end, it is this blueprint that should be matched to the picture of the manifested house.

Integrity is the structural architecture of the house, to fortify it and give it longevity, protecting it against the harsh elements and weather conditions. Time management is the strategic projection of completion for the house by phases; each phase should be managed appropriately, also factoring in the correct seasonal timing for completion of each phase. Finally, Your Contribution is the physical completed house. In other words 'The Big Picture'. A tangible representation of how this house will serve you and others, its ultimate purpose and how it will outlive you.

The remarkable words in Kathy Tricoli's song "Go Light Your World" capture the essence of a life worth dreaming, creating and living for: "Carry your candle, run to the darkness, seek out the helpless, confused and torn. Hold out your candle for all to see it. Take Your Candle, Go light Your World".

A candle does not diminish its own light by lighting other candles. It only enables the room or pathway to become brighter for all. So arise and let your light shine! Let it shine into the dark places of this world. It is time! Hold your corner, take your place, let your voice be heard, let your footprint be seen, make your mark, leave your legacy. Aspire to inspire before you expire. Plan to make your mark in this world, not to leave it stained.

I am now on a mission to spearhead a "Success Gravity" Movement to help you discover how to create something significant and uniquely different that will catapult you towards reaching your goals. The mission is to enable you to discover a new sense of confidence, passion and purpose. It will create a platform for connecting and networking with powerful people making influential impact, as well as infuse you with the RIGHT tools, the RIGHT information and the RIGHT strategies to take charge of every area of your life. This will also help you tap into what's been holding you back and move beyond your fears and challenges in order to make radical changes necessary to passionately pursue your goals and succeed.

Success is a cycle. It is a process that has a formula. It starts with Your Goals and ends with Your Contribution to others. This contribution then begins a new cycle of success. I hope you can see that lying within the pages of this book are simple, adaptable truths that you can apply to your life today and begin to watch your dream life unfold into a tangible reality. A dream that You have created. That tangible, Grounded Success that you so earnestly desire, can finally be gripped, firmly rooted and planted in your life, so that it blossoms and flourishes with fruit that will be profitable and pleasurable for generations to come. Then and only then can they truly say of you when you are gone that, "Indeed...Here Lies A Great Ornament To The Human Race".

To Your Success!